• HALSGROVE DISCOVER SERIES ➤

THE SUFFOLK COAST

Philip Morgan

HALSGROVE

First published in Great Britain in 2011

British Library Cataloguing-in-Publication Data
A CIP record for this title is available from the British Library

ISBN 978 0 85704 102 9

HALSGROVE
Halsgrove House,
Ryelands Business Park,
Bagley Road, Wellington, Somerset TA21 9PZ
Tel: 01823 653777   Fax: 01823 216796
email: sales@halsgrove.com

Part of the Halsgrove group of companies
Information on all Halsgrove titles is available at: www.halsgrove.com

Printed in China by Everbest Printing Co Ltd

CONTENTS

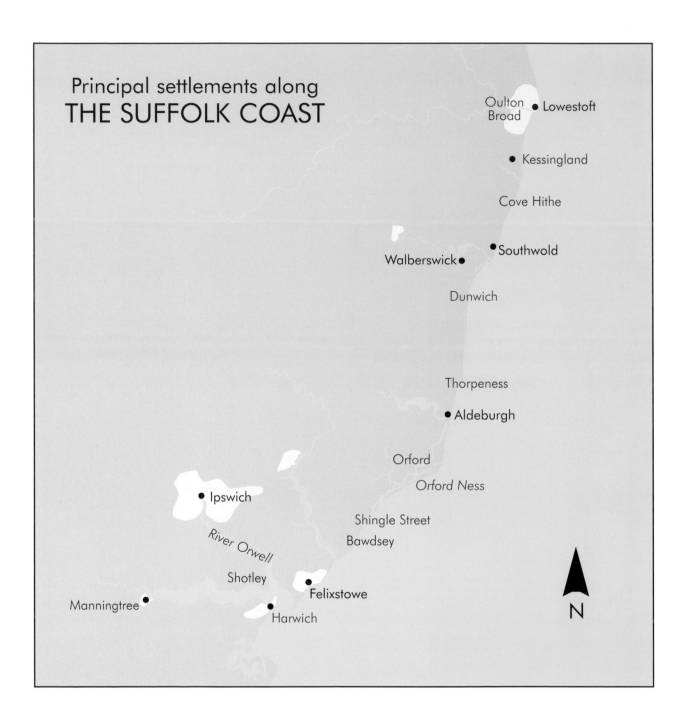

Principal settlements along
THE SUFFOLK COAST

Oulton Broad
● Lowestoft

● Kessingland

Cove Hithe

Walberswick ●
● Southwold

Dunwich

Thorpeness

● Aldeburgh

Orford

Orford Ness

Shingle Street

Bawdsey

● Ipswich

River Orwell

Shotley

● Felixstowe

Manningtree ●

Harwich

N

Pin Mill

Buttram's Windmill

INTRODUCTION

THE SUFFOLK COASTLINE is well known for its quiet beauty and with a mix of seaside resorts, ports, hidden beaches and coves, river estuaries, heaths and forests there is plenty to explore and discover.

The area has a diverse and interesting history. It has strong Roman connections, while the well-known Anglo Saxon burial site at Sutton Hoo, close to Woodbridge, found just before the outbreak of World War Two, is widely recognised as among most significant archaeological find in the country. The Suffolk coast has also seen its fair share of invasions and the castles at Orford Ness and Framlingham, a few miles inland, are a sign of the threat Suffolk faced in the eleventh century. Other major buildings reflect the wealth of the area resulting from agriculture and wool in medieval times. Over the passing centuries such threats of attack from overseas have been of constant concern and during the sixteenth century the Dutch posed a challenge with fierce battles fought against them at Lowestoft in 1665, Landguard Fort at Felixstowe in 1667, and the battle of Sole Bay off Southwold in 1672. In the early nineteenth century the danger this time came from France. With the anticipated invasion by Napoleon a line of substantial but relatively simple Martello Towers were built along the shoreline to keep fortified the areas most seen to be at risk from invasion. Today several still stand at Felixstowe, Bawdsey, Shingle Street and Aldeburgh as a reminder of the not so distant threat. More recently World War Two left its mark with industrial towns such as Lowestoft heavily bombed, while at Bawdsey the grand manor house was bought by the Air Ministry in 1936 where the scientist, Robert Watson-Watt, together with a team of scientists developed the first radar system shortly before the outbreak of the war.

The River Orwell is the largest river in the county with the pretty Shotley Peninsula and Pin Mill, once a haven for smugglers and now a popular spot for sailors, nature lovers or walkers. At the end of the estuary stands the historic town of Ipswich, once a prosperous port, as well as the birthplace of Cardinal Wolsey. In recent years the waterfront has undergone significant redevelopment and the town has a number of historical and modern sites of great interest.

The mouth of the Orwell is also the site of Felixstowe, the largest container port in England and one of the largest in Europe, handling a huge amount of cargo every day. Its rise as a port has been relatively rapid, developing quickly from a small and run down site before World War Two to its present size. Landguard Fort, at the mouth of the estuary, has also seen its share of military action, most notably during the seventeenth and eighteenth centuries. Earlier, in Roman times, a fort situated close by served as a lookout for invaders eager to make their way upstream although erosion steadily claimed its last remains in the nineteenth century. Today Felixstowe is a small seaside town attracting many visitors during the summer. Following the coast north, Orford Ness is a tranquil community and a popular location for visitors of all ages, with boat trips out to the ness and lighthouse. The remains of bunkers and research buildings nearby also serve as a reminder of the role the secluded and rather remote parts of the Suffolk coastline played in preparing for conflict in World War Two.

Erosion and the power of the sea have always been a particularly striking feature along this stretch of coastline, and at Dunwich the extent of erosion over the centuries steadily swallowed the whole town. Dunwich was once the largest town in Suffolk and a bustling port but during the thirteenth century its fortunes began to decline. During a powerful storm on 14 January 1328 the harbour was fatally damaged (from which the nearby village of Walberswick, on the mouth of the River Blyth, was able to benefit). Over the passing years whole streets and at least four churches were lost to the waves, along with the remains of an early Roman port as the cliffs steadily crumbled away. Today the shingle beach lies largely deserted with visitors coming to enjoy the scenery during the summer months, with Dunwich Heath and the Minsmere nature reserve close by. Walberswick fortunes as a port continued long after Dunwich's demise, with the last of days of trade ending in the early twentieth century. It was around this time the painter, Philip Wilson Steer, a pioneer of the English Impressionist movement, painted a number of scenes of the village, and of Southwold just across the River Blyth. The village continues to attract artists and, along with Southwold, the area provides plenty of interest for its many visitors.

The sea in many respects has been a mixed blessing for the coastline. Coastal erosion is a growing problem yet the area remains a pleasant holiday retreat for the visitors of today, just as in times past it supported communities through fishing, shipbuilding and other trades. As this book shows, the Suffolk coast has a simple charm and intricate history which makes the coastline well worth discovering.

Chapter 1
RIVER STOUR

THE RIVER STOUR marks the boundary of Suffolk and Essex and this is where I chose to begin my journey around the Suffolk coast. Following the river upstream from its mouth at Shotley Peninsula, with Harwich in the distance across the estuary, the river has a number of sites well worth exploring.

The Royal Hospital School at Holbrook is a particularly impressive building on the banks of the Stour with its distinctive tower and frontage overlooking a large sports field which leads down to the water, providing a pleasant environment for learning. Today it is a well known co-educational public school with boarding and day-school pupils, although it retains some of its traditions and links with its maritime past, most notably with the naval-style uniform worn by pupils on significant occasions.

In 1694 King William III and Queen Mary II founded the Royal Hospital for Seamen at Greenwich in London. The Royal Charter for the hospital included provision for the maintenance and education of the children of Royal Navy seamen who were killed or disabled. The hospital, which once stood on the site of the old Naval College, was built in 1696, and in 1712 the school was founded in Greenwich with the first pupils described as 'ten orphans of the sea' attending in 1715. By 1758 a small purpose-built school was completed at Greenwich with a larger building replacing it in 1782. The hospital, which served as the school's first home, continued to provide a residence for naval veterans until 1869.

Life at school was disciplined and thorough for the pupils. The day began at 5am with an outdoor swim, while the emphasis on arithmetic and navigational skills equipped students well for naval life. As demand for places grew the school needed space to

The impressive school buildings, designed by Herbert Buckland, date from 1933.

expand and in 1933 the school moved to its present 200-acre site at Holbrook beside the Stour. The imposing school buildings were designed by Birmingham architect Herbert Buckland, best known for his attractive Arts and Crafts style houses.

Up until the 1950s the emphasis continued to be on preparing students for a naval career and all boys were required to join the Royal or Merchant Navy. In more recent times it has adapted and continues to be a successful Independent school with approximately nine hundred pupils aged eleven to eighteen.

Bordering on the Royal Hospital School is Alton Water Reservoir. The reservoir is a popular spot for sailing and windsurfing and on summer afternoons visitors also come for a picnic, bike ride or simply to take a walk. A Royal Yacht Association registered school is run at the reservoir, although the generally quiet environment also allows a variety of wildlife to enjoy the surroundings, with butterflies, dragonflies, and wildfowl living around the water.

Sailing and water sports on Alton Water.

The reservoir was officially opened by Princess Anne on 13 July 1987, providing Ipswich and south Sufffolk with water.

*Hiring a rowing boat along the
Stour is a popular activity during
the summer.*

By the early 1960s it was realised that the water supply for Ipswich was unlikely to meet
the rising demand in future years and it was decided the solution would be to pump
water from the River Gipping, north of Ipswich, into a storage site at Stutton on the
grounds of the old Alton Hall. In 1974 work started on building the reservoir. London
clay was used along with sand and gravel to construct the 390 acre site with a capacity of
200 million gallons and work was completed by 1976. The next step was to construct a
pumping station at Sproughton to pump the water from the Gipping, this being
completed in 1978. In the early 1980s the process of water treatment then had to be
addressed and this was done using dissolved air and filtration using sand and activated
carbon filters. By October 1986 the reservoir was supplying customers and the final
touches were completed by March 1987.

Just a short distance away is Stutton Hall with its grounds backing on to the river. This
grand house was built around 1553 by Sir Edmund Jermy. It originally had a timber frame
structure although over the next two centuries the house was enlarged and rebuilt with

brick, and is particularly notable for the ornate chimneys. The house, set in pleasant surroundings, is privately owned. Following the river on we come to the small village of Brantham, while close by at Cattewade the Norwich to London railway line crosses the river before stopping at Manningtree.

A short distance along the Stour is Dedham Vale. With the villages of East Bergholt and Dedham on the Essex/Suffolk border it is recognised as an area of oustanding natural beauty, better known as Constable Country. Time seems to stand still here, the landscape seemingly unchanged and largely familiar from the scenes depicted in John Constable's paintings, with the river meandering gently along and cows grazing in the meadows. The bustle of modern life feels like a distant memory and it is easy to forget the busy A12 is just a few miles away. The artist Thomas Gainsborough, born in Sudbury a few miles along the Stour, also drew inspiration from the river, as have many other artists since. The famous equestrian painter Alfred Munnings also lived in Dedham and his former home is now a hotel displaying a number of his paintings.

Dedham was a prosperous town in the sixteenth century, growing rich from wool which was transported in barges on the river nearby. Today many of the wooden beamed and

A colourful garden in the centre of Dedham village.

14

later Georgian buildings provide the village with a sense of character that is held in high regard by visitors and locals alike. On my visit, walking along the main street, gardens are in full bloom with bees busy in the sunshine. The village is dominated by the imposing church of St Mary the Virgin, its 131-foot tower providing a timeless presence in the landscape, just as it appeared in a number of Constable's paintings, in all featuring in twenty-six of his pictures.

The church of St Mary dates from 1492 with the construction of the building completed by 1522. The tower itself is an independent structure, completed in 1519, and it is thought its construction may have been funded by the mother of Henry VII, Margaret Beaufort. Inside the light atmosphere with its attractive stained-glass windows is further enhanced by Constable's painting 'The Ascension', one of three religious scenes he created, making the church well worth a visit. A church has stood on the site since at least 1322 although the earlier building was rather smaller and founded on the site where the south isle chapel now stands. But as with many local villages, the growing prosperity of Dedham was reflected in the building of the new church.

Just across from the church is the Marlborough Head Inn which also dates from the sixteenth century and today is remains a busy pub and a popular meeting place for

The church of St Mary dates from 1492 and appears in several of John Constable's paintings.

The Marlborough Head Inn is a popular stopping off place for visitors enjoying the scenery along the Stour.

Flatford Mill was once owned by John Constable's father and forms the centrepiece of several of his most famous paintings.

visitors to take a break after a walk by the river. Dedham also has an interesting American connection. Many former residents had chosen to emigrate to the USA during the early seventeenth century and in 1636 the town of Dedham, Massachusetts was founded. Links between those early settlers and the original village have remained strong.

John Constable was born in the village of East Bergholt on the Suffolk side of the river in 1776 and his iconic pictures of the landscape such as 'The Hay Wain', 'Dedham Vale' and 'The Cornfield' along with many others, capture the idyllic way of life in the Stour valley and the beauty of the landscape is still clearly visible.

Following the path by the river as it winds its way towards Flatford Mill with the occasional swan or duck gliding by and dragonflies hovering by the water, and only the sound of a rowing boat in the distance, makes a very relaxing walk. It is easy to appreciate what drew Constable to capture such scenes in his paintings; the quiet tranquility disturbed only by birdsong. In one of his letters he wrote of his fondness for the area to an early painting tutor, John Dunthorne: 'I love every stile and stump and every lane in the village, so deeply rooted are my early impressions,' and he returned whenever he could to sustain himself while studying in London. Later, while living in Hampstead with his wife Maria and their children, he still returned to the Stour valley, and the landscape of his childhood was to remain a permanent source of inspiration

After walking along for some distance we come to Flatford Mill, made world famous by the numerous paintings in which it appears. The mill itself is a hive of activity in the summer bringing tourists from all over the world to see the well-known landmarks, including Willy Lott's Cottage, the scene featured in the Constable's most famous work 'The Hay Wain'. The cottage itself dates from the late sixteenth century and was the home of the farm labourer, Willy Lott, who was born and lived in the cottage for over eighty years and is thought to have only left it for four days during his life.

The cottage owned by the labourer Willy Lott looks much as it did in 'The Hay Wain'.

By the early twentieth century the cottage and mill had fallen into a dilapidated state but after restoration work by the National Trust it now looks as it must have done in Constable's lifetime. The scene itself has altered slightly from that depicted in his paintings, with the loss of the trees to the side of the pond but, while the water level has risen gradually over time, the setting itself is largely unchanged.

Flatford Mill was built in 1733 and in John Constable's time his father, Golding, ran and owned the mill while his son pursued his interest in painting. The family continued working the mill until 1846. It has belonged to the National Trust since 1946 together with Willy Lott's Cottage and all the houses around it, including Valley Farm which dates from the early fifteenth century, and Bridge Cottage from the sixteenth century. The mill itself has been used by the Field Studies Council since 1946 providing courses on botany, conservation and a range of other subjects. A small museum near the mill provides useful information about the area and Constable's paintings. Thousands of visitors come annually to see the famous landmarks or hire a rowing boat for some fun on the river.

John's father, Golding, was a prosperous miller and businessman with influence. Aside from the watermill he owned two windmills which once stood in East Bergholt, and he traded in coal and corn from Mistley, which at that time was a busy port. He was keen for John to carry on and progress the family business but John's love of art led to some conflict with his father, although his mother was more supportive offering encouragement during his early career. On the river the young John would watch the barges pulled by horses plodding along the towpath and negotiating Flatford lock which allowed vessels to travel along the Stour, a scene so attractively portrayed in 'Flatford Mill' painted in 1817. Willow trees have grown by the lock changing the picture we see today. His father's mill at work fascinated John and and his last piece completed before he died was a mill scene, 'Arundel Mill', now found in Toledo, Ohio.

Walking on across the river and up the hill, approximately one and half miles from Dedham (although the scenery makes it seem far less), we come to the quiet village of East Bergholt where Constable was born, baptized and lived as a young man. Following the path provides the opportunity to look down over the vale and survey the scene as Constable must have seen it, with only the sound of blue tits, bullfinches and other birdsong to be heard, although even today the precise location of some of his paintings is a mystery. Arriving in the village, the church, also dedicated to St Mary, is an interesting building its flint walls giving an indication of its age. It is thought to date originally from 1350 and is plainly the oldest building in the village. Particularly unusual and intriguing

The studio where Constable completed many of his famous works as a young man.

is the fact the church has no tower. Towers, like those at Dedham or Lavenham were built to reflect the prosperity of the area but in East Bergholt the falling wealth of the Catholic church during the reformation meant that funds were never available to build a grand tower and a more modest building was left in its place.

A few yards farther on is the site of Constable's childhood home, clearly marked by a small plaque on the railings, although unfortunately the original house has long since been demolished and a modern house now stands in its place. Crossing over the road, hidden quite down a side street, we find the small studio where Constable created his first paintings which were sold in 1803. It is easy to imagine the young Constable making the short walk down the hill to paint his father's mill at Flatford, or setting up nearby, finding inspiration all around so close to where he grew up. The peaceful, idyllic scenery has imbued his work with an enduring appeal. The studio, luckily, has survived in good order and a small plaque serves as a reminder of its significance, as well as indicating Constable's difficult and humble beginnings. His early career proved very hard with recognition of his work as a superb landscape painter taking years to achieve. Indeed he

An attractive house and garden in the centre of the village.

did not sell his first landscape until he was thirty-nine years old. In later life his reputation grew but it was only after his death that his genius was recognised and his work became far more highly sought after. East Bergholt today is a small, pleasant village and after exploring some of the colourful gardens, the church and other sights, we now follow the route back to the river.

THINGS TO DO

- Visit Dedham and the church of St Mary and take a walk around the village.

- Walk along the river towards Flatford Mill and take in the river setting or hire a rowing boat.

- Visit the mill and Willy Lott's Cottage and continue up the the hill towards East Bergholt, looking out for Constable's former studio.

- Visit Alton Water or enjoy watersports on the reservoir.

Chapter 2
THE RIVER ORWELL
AND SHOTLEY PENINSULA

THE RIVER ORWELL is the biggest river in Suffolk and has played an important role in the development of the county, its industry and history and on a bright, sunny day the estuary leading to Shotley is a pretty, often peaceful, place to explore.

The Orwell is probably most well known for the imposing concrete Orwell Bridge which is a considerable and functional, if perhaps not pretty structure. At nearly a mile long it passes over the River Orwell at the edge of Ipswich. Construction began in 1979 and since 1982 it has been a local landmark humming with traffic passing along the A14 to Felixstowe and up the Suffolk coast and beyond. The Orwell is thought to have been named by the Anglo Saxons although until quite recently it was relatively unknown, as Daniel Defoe demonstrated in his 1724 *Tour Through the Whole Island*

The Orwell is a peaceful setting, home to a variety of birds and other wildlife.

The imposing bridge over the River Orwell was completed in 1982 and today is busier than ever.

of Great Britain which followed his journey around England and Wales. As Defoe says 'a traveller will hardly understand me, especially a seaman, when I speak of the River Stour and River Orwell, for they know them by no other names than Maningtree-Water and Ipswich-Water'. Further upstream into Ipswich the non-tidal section is known as the River Gipping, the source of the Orwell, which runs through the town and on to its source at Stowmarket.

Famously George Orwell, although familiar with Southwold, used the river for his pen name. In the past, the river leading to Ipswich was an important route for ships going to the docks which provided much of the industry in the town, although over time the number of large ships has declined and the waterfront and harbour areas of the town have seen much redevelopment in recent years. The old warehouses have been demolished and today it is full of sailing boats and yachts passing along the river for pleasure, with the occasional ship stopping off at the small port which still exists. The estuary is haven for a variety of birds and other wildlife which enjoy the river setting. Overlooking the banks of the Orwell, with a superb view of the landscape, is the intriguing sight of Freston Tower. Hidden away by trees and undergrowth, many locals or visitors are completely unaware of this unusual building. Dating from the sixteenth century, the six storey Tudor tower is reputed to be the oldest folly in England and its spiral staircase is surely worth climbing for some amazing scenic views. Its exact use and history is rather obscure, the novel written by Reverend Richard Cobbold in 1850 only adding to the interest. His book entitled *Freston Tower,* believed to be largely fictional, focuses on the character Lord de Freston and his daughter Ellen, for whom he built the tower so that she could study a different subject on each floor. Its exact date of construction appears also to be a matter of some debate even now, with claims it was built in 1578 by Ipswich merchant Thomas Gooding whereas others have suggested it was built around 1564 or even 1655. For anyone looking at the tower today, its peaceful location, with views of boats sailing along the river, seems ideal for anyone seeking a peaceful retreat or suffering with ill health. Indeed between 1772-79 one of its uses was as a place of recovery for those inoculated against smallpox. More recently, until 1999, the tower was owned by Clare Hunt but as with any old building the maintenance and restoration costs were considerable and she then decided

The unusal sixteenth-century Freston tower has superb views of the Orwell

Two views of Woolverstone Hall, designed by John Johnson and completed in 1776.

to give the tower to the Landmark Trust, a charity set up to restore buildings with the intention that holidaymakers could stay in them. By 2004 it was available to rent.

A short distance further on is the village of Woolverstone with its marina overlooking the river and most notable for the imposing house, known as Woolverstone Hall. The hall, like many other old buildings, has its own interesting story.

In 1773, after protracted negotiations over several years, the land was acquired by William Berners, a prosperous London banker who had plans to build an ornate family home overlooking the river. Shortly afterwards, John Johnson, who had also been responsible for designing and building Berners Street in Marylebone in London for William Berners, drew up plans for the house. Woolverstone Hall was completed in 1776, and with its 60 acres of land it formed an impressive stately home. In fact Berners also owned much of the peninsula, including land in Chelmondiston and Shotley, totalling 6042 acres in all. Over the years several generations of the family were to live in the house.

In 1783 after only a few years in his house, William Berners died. His son, Charles had an impressive obelisk built alongside the riverside as a monument. At 96ft in height it was a considerable column structure topped with a globe and rays. Unfortunately, after standing for many year the obelisk was destroyed accidentally by fire in 1945 during the period the Royal Navy were using the site. Only photographs of this ornate structure remain as a reminder of its grandeur.

Famously the Berners used a mascot, known as the Berners' monkeys, which along with their crest adorned the grounds. For the family this crest held a real significance; the loyal family pet monkeys on one occasion alerted the Berners to a fire in the house and only their calls prevented the fire causing considerable destruction. When the family finally left the house, moving to Wiltshire in 1937, they took their valued crest with them.

In 1937 the house was acquired by Oxford University as an investment but by the 1950s the Greater London Council (GLC) wanted to use the site for a council boarding school, with children from London coming to be educated in the rural surroundings. In 1958 the Council bought the site and spent £250 000 developing it, after which it became known as the 'Cockney Eton' and by the 1970s it had grown considerably. By 1977 however, the management of the school had lost direction, discipline was poor and an Ofsted report in 1985 was particularly damning. The days were numbered for the school and despite some protests, it eventually closed in 1990. Today the house is the setting for Ipswich High School for Girls which moved to the site from the centre of Ipswich in 1992.

Just a short distance from the house is the small church of St Michael, built alongside the house in 1776 by John Johnson for the Berners family. By 1860 the church was in need of some attention and Sir George Gilbert Scott carried out repairs to the structure and rebuilt the chancel. In 1889 the nave was rebuilt by J P St Aubyn.

The village of Woolverstone dates back to at least Saxon times with two mentions in the 1086 census, a time when Ipswich and the surrounding area grew considerably. Woolverstone takes its name from Thomas de Wolverston who was the main landowner. This was a period when taxes were being raised for war by King Edward II and the family were remained major landowners in the area for many generations.

This area of the river and Woolverstone in particular is notable for stories of intrigue and tales of smuggling. The 'Cat House', a cottage reputedly built by Charles Berners which overlooks the river, was rumoured to be the setting for the illegal activity. There are stories that a white cat was placed in the window of the cottage to communicate with the smugglers, confirming a safe time for them to come ashore with their contraband.

Sailing boats and barges have long been part of the character of Pin Mill and a busy boatyard continues to operate by the quay.

Inconveniently, sometimes, of course the cat would move and this method was not always effective, but within these quiet surroundings, activities such as smuggling are easy to imagine. Even after the cat died it was stuffed and placed on the window sill as a covert messenger.

About a mile downriver is the picturesque setting of Pin Mill with sailing boats dotted about the bay. The shoreline is looked after by the National Trust and is a pleasant place to spend time and explore the tranquil setting. Arthur Ransome was clearly fond of the charm of Pin Mill and based two of his children's books here, *Secret Water* and *We Didn't Mean to go to Sea.* With the peace of the river, the bustle of the busy town of Ipswich just a couple of miles upstream, seems like a distant memory. The Butt and Oyster is a popular resting place for visitors, with good views of the passing boats and judging by old photographs the scene seems to have changed little in the last hundred years. The boatyard is busily working away on a variety of vessels and in the past played an important role in repairing Thames sailing barges, large attractive sailing boats with dark coloured sails which occasionally are still seen sailing up the North Sea coast.

Following the river for a short distance we come to Shotley, the end of the peninsula and the opportunity to witness the hive of activity going on at Felixstowe just a short distance across the Orwell. Cranes busily unload and distribute containers, with lorries and other vehicles movingly rapidly around the quay, seeming almost to resemble a giant Meccano set at work. Felixstowe today is the largest container port in the UK with a huge amount of goods being imported and exported everyday. Watching vast ships being manoeuvred, unloaded and leaving the port is a fascinating sight.

The view from the peninsula also gives us the chance to understand the setting, with mouth of the Orwell and Stour estuaries and Parkestone Quay and Harwich just across the water from Felixstowe, probably only a few hundred yards away. The North Sea is also visible with ships coming and going, and the north Essex coast on one side and Suffolk on the other. The route invaders took in Anglo Saxon times is clear and it is easy to imagine incomers from Europe or Scandinavia passing along and forming settlements

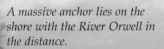

A massive anchor lies on the shore with the River Orwell in the distance.

A barge at dusk near Pin Mill.

Container ships at Felixstowe Port at the mouth of the River Orwell.

in the area a short distance up stream. Shotley, like Woolverstone and Pin Mill, was an important base for the Royal Navy during the Second World War with HMS *Ganges* providing training for navy recruits. Unfortunately the base is now derelict although many of the veterans have fond memories of their time spent here. Recently fortifications from the Napoleonic era have been discovered which, along with the existing Martello Towers and fortifications in Clacton and the Redoubt Fort in Harwich, convey the threat that this area of coastline was thought to be under from France during the early 1800s.

Today this area of the river and Shotley Peninsula is popular for sailing, with visitors enjoying the surroundings and opportunities for exploring.

THINGS TO DO

• Walk around Pin Mill and spend time by the quay or have some refreshments in the Butt and Oyster Inn overlooking the river.

• Visit Shotley and take in the scenery with ships sailing up the Orwell or coming into port at Felixstowe.

• Explore Orwell Country Park and the views of the river and bridge as well as old woodland on the edge of Ipswich.

Chapter 3
IPSWICH

IPSWICH IS THE largest town in Suffolk with much to offer the visitor, whether enjoying the shops and amenities on offer or its sights and history.

Arriving in the town, changes have been taking place rapidly at the Ipswich waterfront, known as Neptune Quay and Haven Marina, the scene of Ipswich's docks which in recent years had become dilapidated and in need of major redevelopment. The docks had been

Yachts and residential buildings now take the place of the former docks.

an integral part of the town since at least the eighth century and a settlement gradually grew up around the quay area with a number of the historic buildings and churches found close by. The town is in fact home to thirteen historic churches in all, a particularly large number for a relatively small town with three just a short walk from the quay and several others dotted about in close proximity. In April 1644 the Puritan William Dowsing visited the town and it took him two whole days to visit all the churches on his campaign of destruction, smashing windows and religious items inside.

When they were built in 1839-45 Ipswich docks were the largest on the east coast, with the main exports of grain, animal feed and fertilizer. In time, as ships became ever larger and the ports of Harwich and Felixstowe developed upriver, able to handle the bigger vessels, the docks at Ipswich gradually declined. The old flour mill and other industry is now mostly gone from the quay, with demolition, restoration and building on-going in recent times, gathering pace since 2006 with large sums spent to regenerate the area. The old R & W Paul Maltings building close to the passing traffic is the last reminder of a busy industry which used to take place at the quayside. Pauls began producing speciality types of malt and photos from the 1920s show a rather different scene with a fleet of barges in the dock which the company used to run, transporting the malt from the port to breweries in London. Today the company still operates from Stowmarket and Bury St Edmunds and has a sole surviving barge, the *Etna*.

One of the best-known industries in Ipswich was the Ransomes Company which produced a range of lawnmowers and other agricultural equipment in the town until 1987. Today the only reminder of the once large industry is the Ransomes Europark industrial estate close to the A14. Robert Ransome was born in 1753 and in 1785 started a brass and iron foundry in Norwich, one of the earliest in East Anglia, and began producing plough shares. By a fortunate mistake he discovered a process known as chilled casting when a broken mould in the foundry caused molten metal to come into contact with cold metal which resulted in a very hard and durable metal being produced. This proved ideal for ploughs which he marketed as 'self sharpening'. He patented his discovery and the business quickly grew, selling parts through fifty outlets in Norfolk and Suffolk.

In 1789 he moved to Ipswich and brought one workman with him, establishing a foundry in an old malting as the business continued to grow. His sons followed him into the business but with the Napoleonic wars the market for agricultural equipment declined. In 1812 the clever Ipswich engineer William Cubitt, who was later knighted and became President of Society of Civil Engineers, joined the firm. Ransomes then began to move

Ipswich waterfront and Neptune Quay is now home to a large marina as well as the distinctive university buildings.

into cast iron production and in 1818, after a severe flood washed away Stoke Bridge in Ipswich, the town corporation asked Cubitt to design a new cast iron bridge which once constructed lasted for over a hundred years. As well as the bridge, Ransomes were also responsible for constructing the first gas works in town and the business continued growing in stature.

In 1830 the first lawnmower had been invented by the clever engineer, Edward Budding, who came up with idea from a cylinder cloth-cutting machine he had used while working for his employer, John Ferrabee at Phoenix Works, Gloucestershire. Edward worked secretly in the evenings to perfect his invention, although despite gaining a patent he lacked the funds to develop his mower idea further and there is little evidence that he gained financially from his efforts. In 1832 the first mowers of his design were produced under licence by Ransomes and by 1852 fifteen-hundred mowers of the Budding design had been produced. Meanwhile agriculture was also beginning to thrive again and during the 1840s Ransomes began making steam engines as well as over three hundred types of plough and other machinery. They were given the first gold medal to be awarded at the Royal Agricultural Show, held in Liverpool in 1841, with one of their impressive portable steam engines proudly on show. In the same year, and with the growth of the railway, the company moved in a new direction and James Ransome and Charles May began working together and patented a new device known as a trenail and chair which was used for fastening rails, enabling new railway lines to be rapidly laid. These devices could be quickly mass produced and, made of chilled iron, they proved very profitable for the firm.

With this growth in production the new Orwell works was built on Ipswich Quay and by 1849 the old foundry had been closed, with a great feast held for the employees to celebrate the event. In 1851 Ransomes was awarded four medals at the Royal Exhibition which had been promoted by Prince Albert, and at the 1864 Royal Show held in Newcastle the company's new design of plough proved successful in the hands of a champion ploughman, James Barker, and the 'Newcastle Plough' was unveiled. In 1867 Ransomes also produced the 'Automaton' lawn mower which was a development of the original Budding design. The new design now had small adjustable rollers at the front to alter the cutting height and, produced in a variety of sizes, the Automaton was to prove very popular for the next thirty years. The growing trend for well-cut lawns and the popularity of sports such as cricket, tennis and golf meant that the mowers were sold in places as far afield as Australia and India and today these early cylinder mowers are particularly highly sought after by collectors. Times were good for the company and by now its wide variety of products were in demand all around the world.

In 1869 the booming railway business was transferred to a new company called Ransomes & Rapier which had been set up by James Ransome, son of the senior partner of Ransomes, also James Ransome. Together with RC Rapier the new company proved very successful in producing railway machinery and manufactured locomotives for the railway in China in 1875. Towards the end of the nineteenth century Ransomes continued to expand with a new lawnmower works opened in 1876 and a growing trade in steam engines in the 1880s.

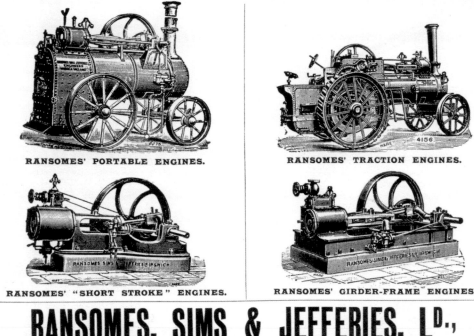

STEAM ENGINES & THRASHING MACHINES.

RANSOMES' PORTABLE ENGINES.

RANSOMES' TRACTION ENGINES.

RANSOMES' "SHORT STROKE" ENGINES.

RANSOMES' GIRDER-FRAME ENGINES.

RANSOMES, SIMS & JEFFERIES, Lᴰ.,
ORWELL WORKS, IPSWICH; AND LONDON, 9, GRACECHURCH STREET.

An advert from 1894 showing a range of steam engines produced by Ransomes, Sims & Jefferies as the company was known at that time.

The First World War was to be a challenging time for the company. Its substantial overseas markets were lost overnight and, instead, it now began producing equipment for war including producing munitions, vehicles and even 350 FE 2 fighter aircraft. The first women employees were also taken on at this time and at the height of production there were 5000 workers. During the 1920s the company continued to diversify to try and make up for lost trade and began producing electric vehicles such as Trolley buses which were exported around the world and were also a popular feature of Ipswich High Street at the time. With the onset of World War Two the factory again had to switch to wartime production and in 1949 it moved to a new site at Nacton.

By the 1970s Ransomes had seen many changes and now concentrated on far fewer products, relying increasingly on its core market of lawn mowers and lawn care. In 1976 it ceased production of its combine harvester, the end of a 130-year association with harvesting and by 1987 it was the largest lawnmower maker in Europe and the third biggest in the world. The end however was in site for the company and the 1990s was to be its last decade when it was bought out by the American giant, Textron, in 1998. Today Ransomes is little more than a memory in Ipswich but the Ransomes' exhibition in the Museum of East Anglian Life in Stowmarket is well worth a visit with details of the companies illustrious past and includes a threshing machine, several of the famous lawnmowers and ploughs and a Ransomes steam engine from 1881.

Another famous industry in Ipswich's past was the Fisons fertilizer company. Fisons traces its first roots back to a fertilizer business formed by Edward Packard in 1843 who was one of the early pioneers of the producing chemical fertilizer by dissolving bones or coprolites in sulphuric acid. He built the first acid and superphosphate factory in the Bramford area of Ipswich in the 1850s. The business prospered and in 1895 it became Edward Packard & Co Ltd. In 1919 the company acquired the business of James Fison of Thetford which had been founded in 1808 and the new business of Packard & James Fison was formed. Competition however grew with increasing imports of superphosphate and in 1929 the company amalgamated with fellow East Anglian competitors, Joseph Fison & Co, founded in 1847, and Prentice Bros Ltd which had been founded in 1856. As a result Fison, Packard & Prentice Ltd was formed. Over the next fifteen years Fisons acquired another thirty-two competitors which were mostly small local businesses and continued to grow. By 1942 it became known simply as Fisons and in the 1980s the business began producing pharmaceutical chemical products and the fertilizer business was sold to Norsk Hydro in 1982. However by 1993 the future of Fisons looked bleak. In 1995 the instruments division was acquired by US Thermo Instrument Systems while the research facilities were bought by Swedish company, Astra AB and Fisons' presence in Ipswich came to an end.

The Old Custom House seen beyond the line of pleasure cruisers.

With the construction of the new and distinctive university buildings for the former Suffolk College and a busy marina, the docks are a picturesque setting well worth exploring. Walking along the waterfront, sailing boats lined up at the quay glisten in the sunlight and with the occasional boat sailing by, visitors pause to take in the scene. Restaurants, bars and other businesses are now taking the place of the old warehouses and have brought life to an area which had stood largely derelict for many years.

Today the most notable building on the quay is the neo-classical Custom House building designed by J M Clark which, when completed in 1844, stood at the centre of the docks

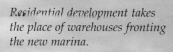

Residential development takes the place of warehouses fronting the new marina.

Modern development by the River Gipping.

during their nineteenth century heyday. The striking red and cream brick design and grand four column portico displaying the Ipswich coat of arms is a reminder of the port's former significance and was praised as 'remarkably original' by the architecture critic, Nicholas Pevsner. The building has also seen some renovation in recent years and today is a Grade II listed building with the ground floor used for conferences and other purposes.   A few yards along the quay is the imposing Jerwood Dance Building, the modern face of the town with its 234ft high, twenty-three storey tower dominating the skyline. The building opened in 2009 at a cost of £8.9 million with a dance and arts academy playing a part in the ambitious regeneration plan.   Many of the other buildings are apartments and residential buildings with development continuing apace. A small dock still exists slightly downriver on the entry to the town with a container terminal capable of handling a variety of cargoes and the occasional vessel can be seen sailing along the Orwell.

Ipswich was originally known as 'Gippeswic' and has a long history, with a Roman fort sited at Felixstowe a few miles up the Orwell, strategically very important. There was also a large Roman villa sited in the Castle Hill area of Ipswich, a couple of miles from the centre and just off Norwich Road which featured in an episode of the 'Time Team' series in 2010. The town has a strong Saxon influence dating from the seventh century, growing from the small but significant port which was well placed for trading with Scandinavia and with access to the Rhine. Trading wool was a major industry along with crafts such as pottery. But with its proximity to Denmark it was susceptible to invasion and was conquered by the Vikings and held from 869 to 917, until it was then taken back by the Saxons. The nearby Sutton Hoo burial site near Woodbridge, ten miles from Ipswich, is further testament to the historical significance of the area and is thought to have belonged to Raewald, King of East Anglia, who died in AD625. A number of well-preserved artefacts were recovered from the buried longboat (including the superb warrior's helmet), of the type common in Sweden. The site was excavated in 1939 and the artefacts are held in the British Museum.

Walking on from the quay towards the town centre is Nicholas Street, part of the old town that has been preserved. On the corner of Silent Street is Curson Lodge, a large Tudor building, characteristically overhanging the street, which in the fifteenth century was a busy inn as the port bustled with life. Today it accommodates a clothes shop and a small plaque denotes the building's significance as the site of the former home of Thomas Wolsey's parents and where he spent his childhood years. The original building unfortunately is now gone although Wolsey is undoubtedly the most famous figure associated with Ipswich.

Thomas Wolsey was born in Ipswich around 1473 and was the son of a butcher and cattle dealer. His father however made provision for Thomas to have a good education and he was able to attend Magdalen College, Oxford. In 1497 Wolsey was voted a full fellow of Magdalen and shortly after he was appointed Master of the school there and joined the church, becoming a priest at Marlborough in 1498 under the patronage of the Bishop of Salisbury. In 1500 he gained a second church post, the Rector of Limington, Somerset, under the Marquis of Dorset whose sons he had taught at Oxford. Wolsey continued to

A young Thomas Wolsey lived in a house by the corner of Silent Street.

gain more church posts and rose in status to become official chaplain to the Archbishop of Canterbury, Henry Dean. When Dean died Wolsey became chaplain to Sir Richard Nanfan. This position was to prove very fortunate for him and Sir Richard noted Wolsey's ability for administration and gave him power to handle his financial affairs and was so impressed he even presented him to King Henry VII. When Sir Richard Nanfan died in 1507 Wolsey joined the royal court as one of the chaplains and quickly attracted the attention of the influential Bishop of Winchester, Richard Fox. Henry VII was aware of Wolsey's skills and began to use him for diplomatic duties, sending him to places such as Flanders. To the King's surprise he travelled and returned home with the business completed within three days. Wolsey continued to acquire a large number of church posts and was given the significant position of Master of the Rolls and he initiated reforms which improved the running of the court of administration. When Henry VIII came to the throne Wolsey continued to gain prominence and the new king was also quick to recognise Wolsey's abilities and continued to give him administrative duties although in time he also received political power both domestically and internationally. Wolsey's growing influence brought financial rewards and this was reflected in York Place which he acquired, as well as a lavish palace he had built at Hampton Court. In 1514 he became Bishop of Lincoln and the next year was given the position of Archbishop of York, later to be Cardinal. On Christmas Eve 1515 he was given his most powerful position, that of Lord Chancellor and by now he was an extremely influential and important figure to Henry VIII. In 1521 Wolsey even had ambitions to become Pope after Leo X died but failed to secure the necessary votes. Wolsey, however, by now was becoming unpopular in England for his extremely extravagant lifestyle, power and for imposing new taxes. With Henry's attack on the monasteries Wolsey began their dissolution in 1528, a process continued fiercely by the King in 1536. The Cardinal's relationship with the King however had begun to sour as Wolsey diverted money which was spent on Oxford, angering Henry VIII. Wolsey's reluctance to further the King's divorce from Catherine of Aragon or gain the support from the Pope was to prove his downfall in 1529, when he felt the full wrath of Henry VIII. The impressive palace at Hampton Court which took the King's eye was seized and Wolsey was charged with high treason in 1530. His health however had now begun to fail and he died on the journey from York before he could be tried.

In the same street are several other historical timber-framed buildings from the same period and it is definitely worth taking time to explore. In stark contrast the large and striking Willis Faber and Dumas office building is situated just a short distance away across a parking area, reflecting the mix of old and new in the town. This was the now famous, Lord Norman Foster's first notable building and is now Grade I listed. Built in

The Grade I listed Willis Faber and Dumas building, designed by Lord Norman Foster, was his first significant project.

With its ornate pargeting the Ancient House is a notable feature of the town centre.

1974 it has been an eyecatching and immediately recognisable feature of the centre since its completion, and to passing motorists or pedestrians walking by it divides opinion and is certainly distinctive. Today Lord Foster is most well known for his role as architect of the 'Gherkin' or Swiss Re tower as it is officially known in the City of London which is now a modern landmark, as well as the impressive Milau Viaduct in France. With its darkened glass and transparent nature the Willis building has an unusual quality and is clearly quite different from the usual office block, with abstract reflections produced on the mirror-like surface, as well as exposing those busily working inside, with its open-plan format, a novel feature for the time. A roof garden with small hedges around the perimeter completes the building providing a small retreat high in the middle of the town.

Walking on further is the Ancient House or Sparrowe's Hall building as it is also known, just off the main shopping street and overlooking the modern Buttermarket shopping centre. This impressive building is particularly interesting for the pargeting and decorative plasterwork depicting various scenes. It dates from the fourteenth century with the earliest recorded owner being Sir Richard of Martlesham, a local knight. In 1603 the Sparrowe family bought the house and the ornate frontage of the building as seen today was added by Robert Sparrowe from 1660-70. In all, several generations of the family were to live in the house over a three-hundred-year period. In recent years it has been a Lakeland Plastics shop although not so long ago was a busy bookshop and has been owned by Suffolk County Council since 1980. At the time, the house was in urgent need of restoration with woodworm and rot but by 1984 work had begun to thoroughly restore it to its former glory and today it continues to be an integral part of a busy shopping street.

The main street is busy with shoppers and the bustling market is a popular feature of the town and takes place outside the grand Town Hall which dates from 1868 and backs on to the Corn Exchange from 1882, which together are the focal point of the town, with a variety of functions and other business taking place inside.

Walking down the main street there is a collection of shops, with the White Horse Hotel a short way down. Today it is a fairly anonymous building to many walking past but it has its own fascinating past as the place where Charles Dickens stayed in 1835. At the time he was reporting for the *Ipswich Chronicle* for a local election. The locals and tradesmen gave him inspiration for some of the characters in chapter 22 of *Pickwick Papers* although Dickens does not recall his stay in the hotel with fondness. Unfortunately many of the other old buildings which existed in the town have sadly been lost amid the demolition which has taken place in the town over the years.

Christchurch Mansion was completed in 1550 and stands at the centre of the park.

A short distance away and slightly up the hill is Christchurch Park, another significant and historic site and one of the best known features of the town. The trees and grounds are especially eyecatching with a variety of large and impressive trees, including oaks, beeches, planes and pines. Some of the trees are obviously several hundred years old with very wide, knotted trunks, and the two ponds with a number of resident ducks and other birds make this a pleasant place to take a break. The park itself is very large, occupying 78 acres in total and it is popular spot for all ages. The site housed an Augustine priory dating from the twelfth century although unfortunately with all the destruction which took place under Henry VIII the monastery was seized and dissolved in 1536 with no trace remaining.

On the site of the former priory of Holy Trinity, near the park entrance, is the most famous feature of the park, Christchurch Mansion, an impressive red-brick Tudor house. A large tract of land here was purchased by a wealthy London merchant, Paul Withipoll in 1545 and the mansion was built by Edmund, his son, shortly afterwards from 1548-50. The ground floor remains much as it was when it was built, and when his granddaughter Elizabeth Withipoll married the sixth Viscount of Hereford, Leicester Devereaux, the mansion passed to the Devereaux family who added the Flemish gables in the seventeenth century and rebuilt the upper floors after a fire in 1670. In 1734 Claude Fonnereau of the well-known Ipswich family, bought the house from Price Devereaux, the tenth Viscount of Hereford.

The mansion continued to be owned privately until eventually in 1892 it was bought by Felix Cobbold, part of the famous brewery family. Felix was also the Mayor of Ipswich. He had become concerned following reports that the house was to be demolished and after negotiations with the Ipswich Corporation he bought the house, safeguarding its future as well as providing funds to build up an art collection inside. The house and park then became public, opening to visitors 1895.

Inside the mansion is a museum with a collection of interesting historical items as well as works by John Constable and Thomas Gainsborough and is certainly worthy of a visit. Both these artists are associated with the nearby River Stour and in 1752 Gainsborough moved to the town, having painted many of the notable figures in his home town of Sudbury. Here he painted portraits of local gentry such as members of the Sparrowe family and businessmen who had grown rich from the thriving port. His career continued to progress and he became a member of the Royal Academy in 1768 and moved to a property in Pall Mall, London in 1774.

The park is a relaxing retreat, close to the bustle of the town.

Just outside the park is St Margaret's Church which dates from the twelfth century and is still in constant use today. Also close by is a monument to the Ipswich Martyrs, nine people who were put to death for their Protestant beliefs in the centre of the town between 1538-68. In 1644 the infamous Matthew Hopkins, known as 'Witchfinder General', put Widow Lackford to death for being a witch. Hopkins also operated in Essex and stayed in Mistley by the River Stour condemning several suspected witches to death. Even today his life and work is shrouded in mystery. Through the park and up the hill we come Ipswich School with its tall tower overlooking one side of the park. The school, originally known as Cardinal College of St Mary, was founded by Thomas Wolsey in 1528 in his home town as a rival to the established and elite schools of Eton and Winchester. For many years it has been a well-respected public school which in recent years has become co-educational and adapted to modern changes in education.

THINGS TO DO

- Walk around the redeveloped docks and marina and continue on to Silent Street.

- Look out for the distinctive Willis Faber building and continue on to the Ancient House building and town centre.

- Visit Christchurch Mansion and park.

Chapter 4
FELIXSTOWE

FELIXSTOWE TODAY is best known as the largest container port in the UK and one of the biggest in Europe but not so long ago the town's fortunes were rather different and primarily it was a busy coastal resort, thriving on the Victorian interest in seaside holidays.

Looking across the River Orwell from Shotley, it is possible to get a sense of the hive of activity going on at the port. Cranes busily unload and distribute containers in all directions and lorries or other vehicles scurry around the quayside.

Felixstowe today is one of the busiest container ports in Europe.

Beach huts sit alongside the Martello Tower on Felixstowe seafront.

A huge quantity of goods are imported and exported everyday and the chance to watch some extremely large ships being manoeuvred by tugs, unloaded and leaving the port is interesting to observe as they sail serenely in and out. As a significant port however, its history is quite surprising. Felixstowe Docks first opened in 1886 but by the First World War trade declined and with the economic depression in 1929 the port fell into disrepair, with the addition of bomb damage inflicted during the Second World War.

In 1951 the docks and railway company were purchased by Gordon Parker who had ambitions to develop it as a major port. Reclamation work began in 1964 and by 1967 it had been transformed into the first container port in England. The port grew significantly with the rise in containers as the new means of transport and Mr Parker sold the now bustling site to European Ferries in 1976. In 1987 P&O took over the port and that year it became the first in the UK to handle a million containers, and it has continued to grow and develop since.

Aside from the docks, the town attracts many visitors, with the children enjoying the seafront, pier and beach huts. The promenade makes a pleasant place for a stroll although quite different from the serenity and quaintness of Aldeburgh or Southwold. The pier hints at Felixstowe's former seaside heyday and dates from 1905, built as the third of a trio by the Coastal Development Company which also built the piers at Southwold and Great Yarmouth, providing stop off and excursion points for visitors. A Francis Frith photograph from the famous collection taken by him on his travels shortly after the pier was completed provides a snapshot in time of its impressive scale, and much like the piers down the coast at Walton, Clacton and Southend in Essex, it was built firstly to cater for steamboats. The Coastal Development Company operated boats, known as the 'Belle Steamers' from London Bridge but the growth of the railway during the late nineteenth and early twentieth century meant that the steamboat trade was an industry in decline. Constructed by the Roger Brothers, the pier was, unusually for the time, instead of iron, built from timber known as jarrah and greenheart which was more durable and resistant to marine worms. At 2640 feet in length it was very slightly longer than the pier at Walton, although a long way short of Southend. Like both those piers it also had a narrow gauge railway to transport visitors along its length.

The pier dates from 1905 and evokes Felixstowe's heyday as a seaside resort.

By 1922 however, the Coastal Development Company had gone into liquidation and the pier was sold to East Coast Piers Ltd. With the outbreak of war in 1939, like many other piers it was acquired and sectioned off by the Royal Engineers and it was never again to recover its original stature. The prominent position of the pier was deemed vulnerable to attack and a large part of the pier was sectioned off leaving a 450 feet pier, with the seaward part quickly falling into decline and later demolished. After the war the remaining pier gradually fell further into decline and in recent years has become little more than a small amusement arcade and a shadow of its former self with the end of the pier no longer open. Plans were even drawn up to demolish the pier or more ambitiously to redevelop it but today it stands as a reminder of a busier seaside past.

A settlement at Felixstowe has existed since at least Roman times. Interestingly the name of Felixstowe only seems to have come into existence in the twelfth century and the town was previously known as Walton. Today Walton is a small suburb of Felixstowe but the castle at Walton, built by the Romans as an important defence post at the mouth of the estuary leading to the River Orwell and Stour, would have had clear strategic importance. It covered six acres and in Anglo Saxon times the monks founded a priory here, but by the eighteenth century the castle ruins slid down the cliff and into the sea.

Landguard Fort stands sentinel over the Orwell and Stour Estuary.

Today Languard Fort still stands as a testament to the strategic importance the area had from preventing invaders. Sitting at the edge of the estuary looking out towards the North Sea, with Harwich just a short distance away on the other side of the water, the fort had a very important role in an area which was a prime target for invasion. Indeed Henry VIII originally had a fort built here in 1540 which consisted of some fortifications on the site. Over time these were rebuilt and the present fort dates from 1875. Particularly significant was an invasion by the Dutch fleet on 20 June 1667 with 1500 troops led by Admiral De Reuter, attempting to invade the fort. The Dutch were well equipped with guns which they had bought from the British but a fleet of soldiers inside the fort inflicted heavy casualties on the invaders with cannon and small arms. British casualties were limited to a handful of soldiers although General Nathaniel Darrell was killed in the battle and is recognised in the town of Felixstowe with a street named in his memory.

The fort of today consists of substantial outer walls and what would have been a drawbridge, outer ramparts and collection of rooms for the storage of weapons, gunpowder and shells and various other purposes fundamental to the operation of the fort. There is a large central fortified structure which includes a parade square and rooms overlooking it which would have belonged to officers and more senior figures. A sally

A fort at Landguard has stood since 1540 but the present fort dates from 1875. It is currently under the care of English Heritage.

The entrance to Landguard Fort.

port, a twisting dark tunnel, existed near the entrance and served as a way for soldiers inside to exit the fort and sneak out to attack any invaders. Clearly the fort has seen a significant amount of action and bloodshed and it has a reputation for supernatural activity and a number of ghostly presences which exist. Walking thorough some of the deserted corridors, amongst the small chambers of rooms, and through the caponier area with its strengthened, domed roof, it is easy to see why. The fort even has its own tragic love story of a Portuguese lady named Maria. She was married to the Paymaster Sergeant and had been accused of stealing a valuable silk purse. Her husband absconded at the claims made against his wife but he was arrested for desertion and then shot for his offence. Dismayed with grief, Maria then threw herself from the Chapel Bastion area at the front of the fort.

The weapons and chance to explore what was once a very importance fort make a visit worthwhile and the large cannon in one room overlooking the sea and shingle beach demonstrates the scale of the weaponry involved. The immense cannon weighs 38 tons

This thirty-eight ton cannon took seventeen men to load.

A small, six-pounder cannon from around 1737 found on the beach at Felixstowe.

and took a crew of seventeen men four minutes to load, with shells weighing in at 371kg (812lb), over a third of a ton. When firing the gun the crew had to be given directions where to aim as the bulk of the gun was so immense they were unable to see the target! A smaller, half ton cannon by the entrance is also worth exploring. Known as a six-pounder cannon, it could fire its shell 1600 yards, or approximately a mile, and was found close to the Martello Tower, a short distance along the beach towards the town. However, it pre-dates the Napoleonic era, estimated to be from 1737-67. The fort even served as a base during World War Two and the tall tower looking towards Harwich became a defence HQ in the 1950s. Enemy ships and planes were tracked and it is thought that it could have served as a co-ordination centre in event of a nuclear attack on London. By 1956 the centre was abandoned.

Close by the fort is a popular viewing area where visitors are able to take in the scenery and watch the ships coming and going. Fortunately today, events are more peaceful than they once were and exploring Felixstowe will prove to be a revealing and enjoyable experience.

THINGS TO DO

- Visit Landguard Fort at the mouth of the Orwell overlooking the port of Felixstowe.

- Take a walk along the seafront with its beaches, pier and promenade.

Chapter 5
BAWDSEY

BAWDSEY SITS ON the coast at the mouth of the Deben estuary, with the river winding its way to Woodbridge, a few miles inland. Over the centuries the Deben has gradually altered course while the sea has steadily eroded the coastline despite the building of sea defences and the shingle beaches attempting to hold back the tide. Today it feels like a rather remote part of the Suffolk coast, surrounded by farmland, although it is popular with visitors and with the Felixstowe ferry operating across the river many chose to make the short boat journey to explore what Bawdsey has to offer. With boats dotted around the quay and the waves lapping at the shore it has a simple charm with some interesting history.

The two Martello Towers across the estuary at Felixstowe are a reminder of the military significance this area of coast once held. Built in 1808 the towers were a response to anticipated invasion by Napoleon and were part of a formidable line of fifty-seven circular forts permanently manned by soldiers and stretching along the north Essex and Suffolk coast. After a short walk from the ferry we come to the long shingle beach with sea kale growing among the stones, the waves lashing powerfully and the imposing sight of Bawdsey Manor looking out over the sea.

Bawdsey Manor with its turrets and ornate chimneys was built in 1885 by the stockbroker and Liberal Member of Parliament for South Suffolk, Sir Cuthbert Quilter.

Originally the land belonged to the Earl of Dysart and during the building of the Martello Towers, one tower was built on the site to correspond with those on the opposite side of the river mouth at Felixstowe. In 1873 the estate was acquired by Sir Cuthbert and the disused tower was demolished. In its place he chose to build a grand, if perhaps slightly

Bawdsey Manor was built in 1885 by Liberal MP Sir Cuthbert Quilter

eccentric, Victorian Gothic holiday home on a slight cliff edge just a matter of yards from the sea with fine views. Quilter continued to develop the house as his main home over the next twenty years, adding the towers and facades with echoes of Tudor and Jacobean buildings along with a mix of Flemish, French and Oriental influences. It provided a lavish home for his family and the social functions he enjoyed. In the grounds, stables were built for his Suffolk Punch horses. His wife, Lady Quilter, was a keen gardener and the inspiration behind the formal gardens and a Victorian kitchen garden, as well as the artificial cliff and rockery which was created from brick, sand and cement by James Pulham & Son The stairway at the front of the house and the gazebo were designed by the architect William Eade. In addition to the manor, Sir Cuthbert had acquired 8000 acres of land on the north bank of the river as far as Sutton Hoo, and the area became his own, rather quiet corner of Suffolk. Apart from the famous finds at Sutton Hoo, the small village of Sutton is notable as the place where Mary Sewell was born and lived her early life. Mary was the mother of the writer Anna Sewell, famous for the children's classic *Black Beauty*. Mary was a successful writer in her own right, writing children's bestsellers and poetry and was the first writer to have over a million copies of her work sold for the book, *Mother's Last Words*.

Looking along the shingle beach towards Bawdsey Manor.

In 1936 Bawdsey Manor became a top-secret research establishment for the Ministry of Defence. After World War One protecting the UK from the anticipated threat of attack or invasion became a priority and in 1934 an air defence exercise was carried out which showed the inadequacy of protection at that time. Although the targets and routes were known, it was found over half of any attacking aircraft would be able to get through to their targets successfully. The Air Ministry wanted to develop a novel system to disable aircraft or their pilots known as 'death rays' and sought the views of skilled Scottish physicist, Robert Watson-Watt, supervisor of the National Radio Research Laboratory and descendant of James Watt, inventor of the first practical steam engine. Watson-Watt dismissed any notion of death rays but instead believed that radio beams could be used to bounce off enemy aircraft, detecting them in flight and enabling them to be tracked and intercepted, and he drew up a memo outlining his ideas. These were met with cautious enthusiasm although the Ministry wanted proof such a system would be workable.

Watson-Watt continued work on his idea and on 26 February 1935 both he and Arnold Wilkins successfully demonstrated a system using a BBC transmitter which managed to pick up a bomber being used as a test target. Shortly afterwards in May 1935 Watson-

Watt, Arnold Wilkins and a small team of scientists moved to Orfordness to conduct a series of historic experiments over the sea that would lead to the world's first working radar system. However, it was soon clear Orfordness was inadequate for further research and Bawdsey Manor Estate was purchased for £24 000. By February 1936 the scientists occupied Bawdsey Manor, the stables and outbuildings being converted into workshops. As part of their work immense 240 feet wooden receiver towers were built alongside 360 feet steel transmitter towers and Bawdsey became the first Chain Home Radar Station.

On the outbreak of World War Two a chain of radar stations was in place around the coast of Britain which were to prove invaluable during the war and particularly during the Battle of Britain when the German planes heavily outnumbered the British.

After the war, Bawdsey Manor remained in the hands of the MOD for many more years and was used as an RAF base throughout the Cold War period. By 1990 Bloodhound Missiles was all that remained at the base and on 31st May that year the Bloodhound force ceased operations and the base was to be closed, with all missiles withdrawn to RAF West Raynham in June. On 25 March 1991 the RAF flag was lowered for the last time and the station finally closed on the 31st March. In 1994 it was bought by the present owners, the Toettcher family, and today a language school is also run from the site although the house is not open to the public.

The last of the giant transmitter masts came down in 2000 but photos and exhibits from the station's working days provide an indication how it would have looked in wartime. The Magic Ear Exhibition is housed in the original Transmitter Block which is managed by the Bawdsey Radar Trust and is open to visitors during the year. It tells the story of the development of radar with the Trust's aim of preserving and restoring the site.

THINGS TO DO

- Visit the quay or perhaps catch the ferry across from Felixstowe.

- Take a walk along the beach with Bawdsey Manor overlooking the sea or visit the radar exhibition.

Chapter 6
SHINGLE STREET

FOLLOWING THE ROAD from Woodbridge, Shingle Street is a close neighbour of Bawdsey sited on a secluded part of the Suffolk coastline with a hidden and intriguing past. Heading down the twisting lanes towards the sea the area seems almost deserted. The tranquility of this long stretch of deserted shingle beach looking towards Shingle Street, with the sea shimmering blue in the sunshine and with dragonflies hovering nearby and farmers busy at work in the distance, makes this a perfect place for a relaxing walk or to appreciate some of the hidden beauty of the Suffolk coast.

This part of the coastline is particularly well known for the finely preserved Martello Towers which stand proudly along the shoreline. In 1801 several similar Martello Towers were built a few miles down the coast at Walton, Clacton and St Osyth's in Essex in response to the feared invasion by Napoleon. As the threat grew the decision was taken in 1808 to construct hundreds of these small fortresses around the coastline from Sussex to Suffolk as a means of defence from invasion as the deserted, flat shingle beaches here were considered a prime target for invaders. Soldiers manned the towers which were heavily fortified until the threat subsided. Over the years many of the towers were demolished and lost, although the towers at Felixstowe and Aldeburgh have survived with their historic significance now fully appreciated.

The northernmost tower is situated at Shingle Street, designated with the number AA with W, X and Y towers looking south towards Bawdsey. The settlement at Shingle Street seems to have grown up at the same time as the towers were built in the early nineteenth century when fishermen began to build cottages from driftwood washed up on the shore. The track to Bawdsey from the south was the only link with the outside world and even now the place retains an air of remoteness.

*The deserted shingle beach is a
relaxing place for a walk by the
sea. The Martello Towers are a
reminder of the threat this area
faced during the Napoleonic Wars.*

After the threat from France passed the towers were used as look-out posts by the coastguard, but by 1881 the coastguard had moved into purpose-built cottages at the north end of the beach, although these buildings were bought soon afterwards as a holiday home by the well known Fonnereau family from Ipswich. Close by, also overlooking the sea is the small and distinctive 'German Ocean Mansion', the history of which is obscure. It stands with a group of other cottages built in the late nineteenth century, and these together make up the hamlet.

The area is also notable for the mystery surrounding its role during World War Two. As during the Napoleonic Wars, this secluded stretch of coastline was considered a prime target for invasion and in 1940 the hamlet was evacuated and the beach mined in anticipation. The army used the houses and later the RAF, but the buildings were not well cared for and after the war several angry residents returned to find their homes had been misused and had to be rebuilt.

In recent years events which took place early in the war have also come to light, with claims made for a number of years that the area was in fact the target of a failed invasion attempt by the Germans in August 1940. These rumours have always been denied, with the information kept under wraps by the Official Secrets Act until 2021. But in July 2010 an account emerged in the *East Anglian Daily Times* from Sue Brotherwood whose father, Dennis, was witness to the events and who knew of the events first hand from his brother, Ernest Ambrose. It seems from this story that a force of Germans were obviously very close to reaching the shore when oil or some other explosive substance was used to set the sea alight, preventing their boats reaching land. Clearly this was a very dangerous and harrowing episode and a number of German boats were set alight with bodies reportedly washed up along the shore and down towards Harwich. Ernest Ambrose, who was involved in the operation, described the dreadful smell and sounds of the battle which he said would haunt him to his grave.

THINGS TO DO

- Walk along the beach and enjoy the tranquil surroundings.

- Take a closer look at the Martello Towers and the interesting local wildlife.

Chapter 7
WOODBRIDGE

A FEW MILES FROM Ipswich and within the peaceful River Deben setting, visitors from far and wide come to explore Woodbridge and its history. The Anglo Saxon origins of the area provide the town with a colourful past, famous for the amazing finds at Sutton Hoo nearby in 1939 and now housed in the British Museum; although the town itself has a number of other sites to explore.

Arriving in Woodbridge, the river and small harbour on the waterfront, with the iconic tide mill looking on, provides a classic view of the town. Indeed, there was a settlement in Saxon times due to its use as a port, with the sea a few miles downriver. It grew steadily in significance in medieval times with the ever-growing size of ships. Woodbridge's harbour and quays could cater for these large vessels, capitalising on this increased trade. The rise in prosperity was reflected in its grand abbey, although with the Dissolution of the Monasteries in 1536 it unfortunately fell into ruins. Thomas Seckford, the best-known figure in Woodbridge's past and an eminent Tudor lawyer, became the owner of the ruins and he built a large, impressive residence on the site which today is the co-educational Abbey prep school overlooking the church of St Mary the Virgin. Thomas Seckford was born in 1515 into a prosperous family which owned a large amount of land in East Suffolk. As a young man he studied at Trinity College, Cambridge before becoming a member of Gray's Inn in 1540 and qualifying as a barrister two years later. His legal career progressed and by 1556 he had become Lent Reader at Gray's Inn and soon after he was given the prestigious position of Master of the Court of Requests. The court itself dealt with petitions to the crown made by the poor and it travelled with the Queen on her progress through England, the Master of the Court going with her. Seckford received substantial sums for his work and for attending the Queen and by now he had considerable influence. In 1559 he was made Surveyor of the Court of Wards and Liveries,

The Deben provided Woodbridge's prosperity for centuries. Much of the sailing today is for pleasure.

Once the home of Thomas Seckford, the Abbey is now a school in the centre of the town.

The Shire Hall was built by Sir Thomas Seckford in 1575.

64

working with William Cecil, later Lord Burghley, with whom had been friends since his early days at Gray's Inn. The two men were now also related by marriage and, working together, they had power over some of the largest estates in the land. Seckford also presided over some high-profile treason cases including some members of his own family who had resisted relinquishing their Catholic faith, to his dismay. He also dealt with request for pardons for crimes such as robbery, sheep stealing and piracy. In 1559 Seckford was elected MP for Ipswich and bought land in East Suffolk, Essex and Clerkenwell in London. The family home of Seckford Hall had been left to his older brother but with his rising wealth Thomas bought a grand manor house in the centre of Woodbridge along with a property in Ipswich, and he also built a house in Clerkenwell. He gradually spent more time in Woodbridge and in 1567 Thomas married Elizabeth, the widow of Martin Bowes, and in 1571 he was recognised for his local work becoming Knight of the Shire of Suffolk. By 1575 he moved the local sessions court from Melton to Woodbridge, where he could run legal affairs in the town from the grand shire hall.

Thomas had also had other interests apart from law and from his experience in travelling he became involved in map making. Christopher Saxton, said to be one of Seckford's pupils from his time at the Bar, was recommended to the Queen by him and so was commissioned to create the first county maps of England. Consequently the first atlas of England displayed the coat of arms of both the Queen and Thomas Seckford.

With Seckford's death in 1587, his will provided funds to establish thirteen almshouses for the poor which were rebuilt in the nineteenth century with income from his charity, the Seckford Trust. These still survive today. The grammar school also benefitted by his death and today Woodbridge School continues to be run by the Seckford Trust. As well as Woodbridge he also made significant bequests to the poor of Ipswich and Clerkenwell.

Evidence of Seckford's presence in the town is still clearly visible today. The ornate red brick Shire Hall with its Dutch gables, which dates from 1575, stands proudly in the centre of the town on Market Hill. It still plays an important role as the Town Hall and focus for council business, with the church of St Mary the Virgin just a few yards away. With its 108-feet flint tower and dating from 1453 it was funded by rich merchants in the area.

Inside, the church features an impressive wooden roof and several attractive stained-glass windows as well as the tomb of Thomas Seckford. The porch of the church was built a short time after the tower in 1455 by a bequest on the death of Richard Gooding, along with other donations, and extensive restoration was carried out in 1863. Unfortunately

The Church of St Mary the Virgin dates from 1433.

An historic cottage in the centre of the town.

Right: *The seventeenth century Ye Olde Bell and Steelyard is still a bustling pub today.*

asset stripping from 1536-40 meant a large amount of its former splendour was lost and in 1644 the infamous Puritan, William Dowsing visited the church during his rampage.

Just a few yards away, New Street also features two rather distinctive buildings from Woodbridge's past. The timber-framed Ye Olde Bell and Steelyard inn dates from the seventeenth century and today still does a bustling trade as a pub in the town centre. A large-framed structure hangs out over the road providing the pigeons with a roosting spot but this device was, in fact, a weighing machine capable of weighing farm carts and their loads, a reminder of the town's commercial past. Just along the street, another large, timber-framed cottage, painted red, also from the same period, provides further interest for visitors, as do other numerous well-preserved buildings of the old town which contribute to its prosperous and intriguing character. Close by is the house where John Clarkson, a significant campaigner for the abolition of slavery, lived from 1820-28. John was the younger brother of Thomas Clarkson, one of central figures in the anti-slavery movement and together they made an important contribution in bringing about an end to slavery.

John Clarkson was born in Wisbech in 1764 and began his naval career as a midshipman at just twelve years of age, eventually rising to rank of Lieutenant. During the American War of Independence he fought in the West Indies where he became aware of the true nature of the slave trade. After the war ended he joined his brother in the campaign to end slavery. A number of slaves had gained freedom by fighting for Britain during the war with America and at first they were resettled in Canada. The Government however failed to honour its promise of land and many were forced to return to slavery. John Clarkson however gathered together 1192 of these former slaves in Halifax, Nova Scotia, and organised their migration to a new life in Africa with fifteen ships prepared for the passage to Sierra Leone. The voyage began on 15 January 1792 and on board the captains of each ship were under strict instructions to treat all the travellers with dignity. Unfortunately sickness on the journey meant that sixty-seven former slaves died and John himself was very ill and weak for many weeks with fever. When he did arrive in Africa he served as Superintendent of the new colony for ten months. The new home for the former slaves failed to provide the idyllic new life that had been hoped for, in particular with problems of land distribution and corruption. Despite this John worked hard to resolve these disputes during his stay and was able to gain the goodwill of the people. When he returned to England he was offered a generous new position if he would resign as Governor of the colony but he refused to do so and was dismissed. Despite these pressures he continued to donate money to the colony.

John then married Susan and they moved to Purfleet in Essex and lived in Purfleet House and he took charge of a large estate belonging to the well-known brewer, Mr Whitbread becoming manager of a local lime works for several years. In 1820 John left the company and moved to Woodbridge, where he became a partner in a bank and lived in what is now Barclays Bank which has a small plaque on the wall. His brother Thomas lived just a few miles away and he joined him in the Peace Movement. John lived in the town until his death aged sixty-four in 1828 and is buried in St John's Churchyard.

Walking down to the river, the tide mill is a particularly big attraction and Woodbridge's most famous site. The tide mill was originally founded by the Augustine priory and was working on the site from 1170. In 1227 the monks founded a market which made the Market Hill area the commercial centre of the town which grew slowly and steadily. With the Dissolution Act of 1536 and the destruction that ensued, the tide mill was seized by Henry VIII in 1536, and in 1564 the mill was granted to Thomas Seckford by Elizabeth I. A tide mill works by harnessing the natural power of the tides. Mills such as these were situated in suitable tidal inlets away from direct power of the waves but with sufficient tidal change to cause the water to fall dramatically as the tide goes out. A large millpond was built at the back of the mill which was filled with the incoming tide, trapping the water at high tide behind a sluice gate. The pressure of the water itself within the pool kept the sluices shut. Once the tide had fallen the water was gradually released, driving the water wheel and turning the mill stones used for grinding flour. The mill could be worked for two hours either side of the low tide during which time it could grind about four hundredweight or two hundred kilos of wheat. The power of the sea and tides were even harnessed by the Romans, with early tide mills thought to have existed on the River Fleet and Lea in London. The principal is still in use today with tidal barrages and dams generating electricity.

The present tide mill dates from 1793. The River Deben here has a three-to-four metre tidal range and in its working day there was a large mill pond, water from which was used to drive the water wheel. The mill had a long working life, using the power of the tides until 1957 when the twenty-two inch oak main shaft broke. Then all activity ceased and it closed as Britain's last commercially operated tide mill. The mill pond behind the mill was sold off and became the marina area of today which is home to variety of yachts and sailing boats. The tide mill rapidly deteriorated but in 1968 it was bought by Mrs Jean Gardner of Gifford's Hall, Wickhambrook at an auction. She set about tirelessly restoring the mill to its former glory with help from some committed volunteers and after considerable work it opened to the public in 1975, although it still required a mill pond to

The iconic tide mill is Woodbridge's most famous building.

operate it. Mr Peter Wyllie worked ceaselessly through his retirement with the vision of one day seeing the mill working again and for his efforts he was honoured by Woodbridge Town Council with the Fellowship Cup for outstanding service to the community. Sadly he died five years before his dream was to come to fruition. The small mill pond area at the back of the mill which was completed and opened in 1982, named Wyllie's Pool, is a fitting reminder of his dedication and meant the wheel could be driven once again, bringing the mill back to life. Today the tide mill is one of only two such working mills in the United Kingdom and it is open to the visitors, allowing them to look inside at the workings of the mill and learn more about its history.

A short distance outside Woodbridge stands Buttram's Windmill, a majestic tower mill in full working order. Walking up to the mill it looks truly imposing and is celebrated as the tallest windmill in Suffolk. It is very distinctive in its construction with a tall, brick tower stretching to 61ft to the top of the cap and towering above all the surrounding buildings.

The mill itself has an interesting history, serving as a working mill for many years and finally ending its working life in 1928 when it ground wheat for the last time. It was built in 1836 by John Whitmore of Wickham Market, a well-known and skilled Suffolk Millwright responsible for a number of mills built in the county and the surrounding area and is a fine example of his skill. The mill was designed to grind wheat into flour and was very modern for its time with cast-iron machinery which was strong and durable, and with Cubitt's patent-type sails, designed by the engineer Thomas Cubitt from Ipswich. These new sails were self-adjusting depending upon the strength of the wind and meant that the work of the millwright was eased slightly when working the mill in full flow. The mill was also designed so that each set of gears had a wooden cog meshing with a metal one which meant that the wooden cog could be easily replaced from local resources as it wore out, without the need for lengthy delays in the operating of the mill.

Buttram's mill is open through the year and grinds flour on occasion.

The brick tower alone, stands at fifty feet and climbing the several flights of steps gives the opportunity to view the surrounding landscape from the small and characteristic windows which were built into the windmill sides. Climbing these steps regularly must have been quite an achievement and certainly not easy if you were tired after a long day of work! It is well worth the climb though, with the inner workings of the mill on display and, upon reaching the top, there are several volunteers busy demonstrating the workings of the mill. In operation the mill would work automatically once all adjustments had been made and only two men would be needed to run it, with the miller sending sacks to be hoisted on to carts and his lad at the top of the mill emptying grain into bins or maintaining the many bearings. With a reasonable amount of wind each pair of stones could grind up to 250kg of flour per hour.

This is a windmill that certainly still functions and just a few minutes before I arrive the sails have been moving round at quite some speed. Looking out, it is clear that the surrounding area has changed significantly in the mill's lifetime. Early photos show the mill standing proud and isolated but since then trees have grown and houses have been built nearby. Bryant's Map of Suffolk of 1825 shows that previously another mill stood on the site which then made way for the present mill, although other details are scarce.

Buttram's windmill is the tallest tower mill in Suffolk.

The mill was built for Pierce Trote, probably as a wedding present from his father, a wealthy Woodbridge ship owner, and the mill stayed in the Trote family for several years. Pierce Trote however, died in 1861 and in 1869, John Buttram became the new tenant. In 1877 he bought the mill for £1000 and in the 1880s it was converted to steam power.

Soon after buying the mill John Buttram had to deal with the trauma of three eldest sons being drowned in an accident on Felixstowe Ferry in 1879. Only George, the youngest and then fourteen survived. The mill stayed in the Buttram family until George's death in 1937.

Back on the ground, the presence of the mill is a truly special sight and Betty Whitworth, the owner of the mill and house next door, comes to tell me more. She and her husband Martin have lived here for forty years with the mill in the grounds of the house. Restoration and upkeep of the mill is ongoing, although a considerable amount of restoration was also carried out in the 1980s and 90s. Suffolk County Council provide assistance with the upkeep but, as Betty explains, costs are extensive and without volunteers they would not be able to open the mill to the public. Buttram's Mill is open at specified dates through the year and is well worth visiting, providing a definite highlight of any visit to Woodbridge.

THINGS TO DO
- Visit the tide mill and waterfront overlooking the River Deben. Carry on towards the centre of the town with its Shire Hall and collection of historic buildings.

- Visit Buttram's Windmill at the edge of the town, the tallest tower mill in Suffolk.

Chapter 8
SUTTON HOO

SUTTON HOO, WITH Woodbridge and the River Deben in the distance, is one of the most impressive and well known archaeological finds of the twentieth century and a vivid reminder of the history and significance of Suffolk and the surrounding area in Britain's past. Today Woodbridge is a popular attraction for visitors with its variety of historic buildings, many dating from its prosperous time as a port in the fifteenth century. Sutton Hoo itself however, provides hints of a far longer history and dates back to the sixth and seventh centuries. The site is now in the care of the National Trust with a small visitor centre, providing access to the site.

The Sutton Hoo treasure is particularly well known to those with an interest in Anglo Saxon history and among the finds were the remains of a superb ceremonial

The burial site at Sutton Hoo, now in the care of the National Trust.

The burial mounds at Sutton Hoo which were once the focus of so much attention have now been reconstructed.

helmet, along with a remarkably well-preserved intricate buckle and purse, all now on display in the British Museum. Overlooking the River Deben, the famous burial mounds mark the spot of the finds which have attracted so much attention and investigation over the years, in particular the mound which contained the ship and its famous treasure. Walking around the site visitors can see the now reconstructed mounds, together with an area later used for pagan executions and burials.

The story of the how the investigation began is particularly interesting. In 1926 a large white Edwardian house, known as Tranmer House, with extensive land and gardens was bought by a newly-married and retired officer of the Suffolk Regiment, Frank Pretty and his wife, Edith. For Edith her new home was to prove exciting and intriguing. In 1930, to her surprise, at the late age of forty-seven she became pregnant and gave birth to a healthy baby, Robert. Sadly however, Frank died just four years later and with her small son to look after Edith's health also began to decline. She sought solace in a spirit medium perhaps to make contact with her husband. Encouraged by what she learned from her visits to the medium, along with advice from friends and relatives, Edith felt strongly the need to investigate the large and curious mounds on her land which had given rise to reports of ghostly activity and spectral figures. Edith contacted Ipswich Museum and a local man and interesting character, Basil Brown, self-taught but clearly a keen and dedicated archaeologist, began to dig up parts of the mounds in June 1938 in the hope of uncovering their secrets.

Digging the site was difficult and slow, particularly clearing the soil and preventing several trench collapses which hampered early efforts. After a brief but fruitless attempt at what became known as Mound 1, he began work on the smaller Mound 3. Brown quickly began finding objects hinting that something of importance had been buried here. Further indications made it likely that earlier investigators had been digging on the site, probably with the intention of robbing the it. Brown pressed on and alongside medieval indicators he continued to make finds of other objects including sixteenth century pottery, probably left by the would-be grave robbers. It is believed that Henry VIII authorised that investigations be carried out on the site and this was probably evidence of those earlier attempts.

Word of an excavation spread rapidly and Charles Phillips at Selwyn College, Cambridge quickly realised the significance of the site and after some intervention he realised that despite Brown's efforts more experience and careful exploration was needed. Phillips then assumed position as leader of the excavation and ordered that Brown stop work on

The finely crafted belt buckle was particulary well preserved and is now on display in the British Museum.

Opposite: *The Helmet of Rewald, the King of East Anglia, who died in AD625, is the most famous of the Sutton Hoo finds.*

the site, although by now it was June 1939 with war looming fast. Brown carried on his work and Phillips quickly assembled a knowledgeable team to provide expert help for Brown, with Stuart Piggott and W F Grimes also proving to be key figures in the dig. The finds were beginning to come thick and fast in July events were particularly significant with the discovery of numerous gold objects and ornaments, garnets and other treasures, culminating in the uncovering of the famous ship burial which remains one of the most magnificent archeological finds in Britain.

With the country on the brink of war Mrs Pretty had no hesitation in the finds being given to the British Museum, and after further investigation and a short inquest, the site of the ship was covered with bracken. Identifying who the grave belonged to proved less clear, although after looking at the evidence it was decided this was the site of a king's tomb probably that of Raewald, King of East Anglia from AD599-625, the most likely candidate and owner of the famous helmet. During the war the site was requisitioned as a training base and in 1942 Edith died and the house was sold and the family moved away.

Today the large mounds stand tranquil as they did for so long and the site provides the opportunity for visitors to gain an insight into the investigation and exciting finds which were unearthed on this part of the Suffolk Coast.

THINGS TO DO
- Visit the burial mounds and take a walk around the grounds

- Visit the exhibition on the site with replicas of the finds.

Chapter 9
ORFORD NESS

ORFORD NESS IS twelve miles north-east of Ipswich and its tranquil and remote setting in the Suffolk countryside, surrounded by the wooded areas of Tunstall and Rendelsham Forests, make the hustle of modern life seem like a distant memory.

Orford Castle was built in 1165 commanding panoramic views of the Suffolk coastline and landscape.

Orford is best known for its castle overlooking the Ness with the sea in the distance and a stream of ships passing steadily to and from the port at Felixstowe. The castle dates from Norman times and was constructed in 1165 while Henry II was king. Historically it was one of the most significant castles in England and its vantage point was well chosen for surveying the coast and threats of invasion. During the building process the marshes were drained and Orford then became a thriving port, sheltered from the sea and with a busy trade exporting wool and importing wine.

The castle's importance however, diminished after Henry's death in 1189 and it was captured by King Louis of France in 1216 after an invasion. In 1280 Edward I sold the castle and with the silting of the estuary its fortunes and significance declined. Today, the keep is well preserved and is a popular attraction, although the outer fortifications have disappeared other than some mounds around the tower. The construction of the castle contrasts significantly in style with that of the nearby castle of Framlingham, which also dates from the twelfth century and which has no keep but merely outer walls, towers and some fortifications. Despite their differences these castles provide an indication of the importance and financial power that East Anglia held as the most prosperous region in the country, due largely to agriculture and the wool trade. The tower at Orford is unlike any other in England with twenty-one sides making up the exterior. Originally there was a curtain wall with several flanking towers, similar in design to Dover Castle, although these are now gone, crumbling away in the sixteenth and seventeenth century.

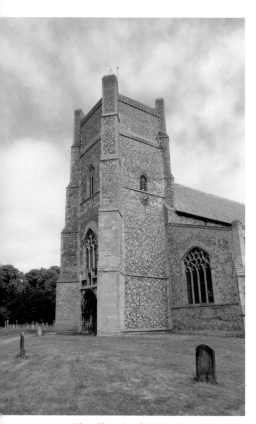

The Church of St Barthomolmew was originally built in 1168. Much of the present-day church dates from the fifteenth century.

Just a short walk from the castle, sits the church of St Bartholomew with its rather distinctive square tower. This too is worthy of a visit. It also dates from Norman times, being constructed at the same time as the castle from around 1165-73. All that remains of the original church is several archways and ruins at the rear of the churchyard. The church we see today was rebuilt in the fourteenth century and this includes the present nave, side aisles and tower. A new roof was added in 1542 but in 1830 the south-west buttress of the tower collapsed and replaced, and further restoration work was carried out on the church in 1890. Today the building is well-preserved although, in common with so many of our churches, work and repairs to the roof are ongoing. Along with the castle it is a popular site for visitors.

The village of Orford itself has a quiet charm. Most of the buildings date from the eighteenth century, many with colourful gardens, and the residents clearly take pride in where they live. Walking on towards the quay, it is busy with sailing boats passing along the Ness, one of the best views of which is taken from the vantage point of the mounds

Today Orford is popular with sailors, tourists and artists.

Boats moored around the Ness with the lighthouse in the distance.

surrounding the castle. Visitors are often seen queuing for the next boat trip that take place hourly around Ness and out to sea, and with a variety of colourful boats moored along the waterfront, and with the lighthouse in the distance, it is a picturesque scene. In the sixteenth century sailing around the Suffolk coastline was fraught with danger, mainly due to the treacherous sandbanks, and until the 1630s shipwrecks were commonplace. For navigation, sea captains often relied on landmarks such as the castle and church, although at night navigation became much riskier. On one stormy night alone in 1627 thirty-two boats ran aground with hardly any survivors.

In 1632 John Meldrum was granted a patent to build two temporary lighthouses between Sizewell bank and Aldeburgh. After assisting many ships in navigating this stretch of coastline the old lighthouses were eventually replaced with the current lighthouse which was built in 1792 by Lord Braybroke of Audley End and designed by architect William Wilkins. In 1965 it became the first automated lighthouse in the UK. It is situated at the end of a thirteen-mile shingle spit between Orford and Aldeburgh and in its time has survived attacks from storms, flying bombs and machine-gun fire. It provides an attractive focal point to the quay although with its remote location it is rather inaccessible to visitors Today however, the lighthouse its under serious threat from coastal erosion which has been taking place at a significant pace in recent years, with the shoreline now just a few yards from the lighthouse. Aerial photographs taken over the last few years clearly show the rapid rate of decline. Early in 2010 Trinity House made the inevitable decision that the lighthouse would not be given protection from the sea due to the estimated cost of £5 million to construct defences and emplace boulders to safeguard its future. Instead, the sea would be allowed to take its course and as a result the lighthouse is likely to be washed away in coming years and the light turned off. Trinity House believe that with modern technology the traditional type of lighthouse is no longer as essential as it once was.

The sailing club has a strong presence in Orford and, as we pass by, is busy with sailors and children enjoying the summer sun, as well as walkers following the path around the bay overlooking the village and the castle. The Ness is an important area for wildlife and the Royal Society for the Protection of Birds (RSPB) operates a nature reserve nearby. For many years it was not possible to visit the Ness but today the National Trust owns the area and trips from the quay operate frequently during the summer.

Looking out across the quay the remains of World War Two 'pagodas' in the distance give a hint of the Ness's hidden past. In 1913 it was acquired by the War Department and the

Ness was drained. A small airfield was constructed and tests were carried out on machine guns and other weaponry, with aerial photography techniques and other important developments undertaken. The operations at Orford Ness were shrouded in secrecy, aided by the quiet and remote location where experiments could take place unnoticed. After World War Two, in the 1950s, the 'pagodas' were built, and it is these odd structures that can be seen in the distance from the quay. These 'pagodas' were in fact test cells for atomic bombs and underground chambers were also built where tests were carried out, although no nuclear material was used. Today these facilities have been transformed into visitor centres and are open to the public providing an insight into military developments which took place here.

After a long and pleasant walk round the quay and bay I decide to walk back and pass The Jolly Sailor, recently voted as one of top three food pubs in East Anglia, and which today is busy with visitors making the most of the village amenities. Orford's history and picturesque charm, its castle and Ness, make it a delightful place for discovering more about the Suffolk coast..

THINGS TO DO

- Visit the castle, in the care of English Heritage

- Walk around the village and then down towards the quay and along the coastal path with the boats and lighthouse in the distance.

- Take an hourly boat trip around the Ness or visit the National Trust site on the Ness.

- Enjoy refreshment at the Jolly Sailor.

Chapter 10
SNAPE

FOLLOWING FROM COAST onwards to Aldeburgh we come to the village of Snape which lies beside the River Alde with marshes and reed beds following the snaking river as it stretches off into the distance.

Snape means 'boggy place' and with the ever-present threat of flooding the settlement moved to higher ground from its original site at the head of the river. Today the village is six miles from Aldeburgh by road although a more sedate twenty-mile journey by river as it works its way out to sea. As with much of the Suffolk coast the area has a long history and in 1862 local archaeologist Septimus Davidson decided to carry out an excavation on Snape Common. His most notable find was the discovery of a grave site which comprised a buried forty-eight-foot long boat probably belonging to a wealthy local chieftain. The non-acid soil in the area meant the find had remained well preserved, although at some earlier point it had already been visited by grave robbers.

Snape is famous for the Maltings and its impressive concert hall, renowned for its excellent acoustics, and which serves as the main venue for the Aldeburgh Festival. The

The Maltings lying beside the River Alde. In 1967 Benjamin Britten moved the Aldeburgh Festival to the site.

festival of music and arts was founded in 1948 by three friends, Benjamin Britten, Peter Pears and Eric Crozier. Britten's fondness for Aldeburgh is well known and inspired by the local surroundings he was keen to provide a platform for young up-and-coming talent. At first the festival took place in churches and village halls but by 1967 the festival needed bigger facilities and Britten and Pears decided to create a permanent home for it at Snape Maltings by converting one of the old maltings buildings into a 832-seat concert hall. Two years later the hall was destroyed by fire but had been reopened within a year. Ambitious to develop their project further, Britten and Pears decided to convert some of the other buildings on the site providing further facilities for the festival and skilled young musicians. In 2006 Aldeburgh Music purchased the concert hall and rehearsal buildings and some of the other maltings buildings to produce new studios.

The Maltings themselves are a reminder of the agricultural significance of the area. By the second half of the eighteenth century East Anglia had become the most important source of grain and other foodstuffs for the London market. The coal and corn merchants, Osborne & Fennell, had originally set up on the site at Snape Quay, by the bridge. In 1841 the site was taken over and converted into a Malthouse by Newson Garrett, grandson of Richard Garrett who had founded the successful enginering works at Leiston. Newson realized early on that his grandfather's business would pass to his elder brother and so was keen to begin his own trade and moved to London to work as a pawnbroker in Whitechapel. While there he married Louisa Dunnell before moving back to Suffolk and building up his business. They were to become a very interesting family and one of his daughters, Elizabeth was the first woman to qualify as a doctor and with her husband, James Skelton Anderson, founded a hospital in London entirely for women. She also became the first woman mayor in England when she became mayor of Aldeburgh in 1908. Another of the daughters, Millicent, married Henry Fawcett, the blind Postmaster General and later became involved in the suffragette movement, becoming president of the National Union for Women's Suffrage Societies.

The first of large malting buildings was built by Newson Garrett in 1846 and he decided, instead of exporting the barley to be malted by the brewer, it would be more profitable to do it himself at Snape. Once malted, the cargo headed down river to London where Newson's son managed a brewery. Only the best barley is used in malting. Originally this was grown locally but as demand grew it was imported from places such as the Danube, Asia, Tunis and Algeria, and even the Pacific coast. Once at the maltings the barley was fed through chutes from the store into vats of water, called steeps, where it was steeped for two or three days before being drained and spread out to germinate on the floors. The process of throwing the wet grain on to the floor, where the germination could begin, had to be done by hand, as with

*The Maltings now includes a
concert hall, a variety of shops
and amenities, attracting
thousands of visitors annually.*

much of the work undertaken. The temperature of the germinating barley was controlled by how it was spread and, after about a week when it had begun to sprout, it was moved closer to the kiln. This chemical change in the barley meant the starch stored in the barley was converted to malt which could later be fermented by the brewer. After germination, an elevator took the wet barley to a floor above the kiln's surface where it was spread and dried until it was the correct colour for each particular type of beer. Stout, for example, required the malt to be heated for longer to achieve a darker colour and different flavour.

The drying process produced a thick mist of steam and, once completed, the sweet, brown malts would be shovelled into a screening loft and shaken and sieved ready for brewing, with the residue used for animal food. Crystal malt which was used to make Guiness and Ovaltine was also made at Snape. This was derived from a longer-rooted type of barley dried out in cylinders rotating over furnaces instead of the method of spreading it out on the floors. The grains of this type of malt resembled grains of brown sugar when split open.

Newson Garett ran the maltings for many years and when he died in 1893 he was buried in Aldeburgh churchyard. His youngest son, George, continued to run the business although it was taken over by S Swonell & Sons of Oulton Broad after World War One. Eventually, modernisation brought an end to the traditional malting methods and sadly Swonell & Sons went into voluntary liquidation. The maltings closed in 1964, quickly becoming dilapidated and signalling the end of a hundred and twenty years of malting at Snape. Then followed the inspirational work of Britten and his friends, breathing new life into the site. Today the maltings is a bustling place with the visitors coming to spend time by the river, enjoying refreshments or visiting the arts and crafts shops. During the Festival Week in June each year thousands flock to enjoy the music and literary events held in the Snape Malting Concert Hall and its associated buildings.

Just downstream is the RSPB reserve at Snape which is a popular choice for birdwatchers with barn owls, kestrels and marsh harriers seen hunting on the marshes as well as kingfishers, avocets, black-tailed godwits, redshanks and many other species.

THINGS TO DO
- Visit the buildings and shops at Snape Maltings

- Take a walk along by the river or head downstream to the RSPB nature reserve.

Chapter 11
ALDEBURGH AND THORPENESS

ALDEBURGH AND THORPENESS are neighbouring communities on the Suffolk Coast and on a bright day they provide perfect places to explore.

Aldeburgh, a Suffolk seaside town with a relaxed pace of life, is famed for its connection with Benjamin Britten, the composer and musician who was resident in the town for several years. He moved here in 1942 and, as mentioned in the earlier chapter, co-founded the Aldeburgh Festival, promoting arts in the area. He died here in 1976. A large and rather unusual house, now painted blue and overlooking the sea, is where Britten first lived, now marked by a plaque. It stands close to the Moot Hall, a distinctive timber-framed building dating from 1560. The hall itself was formerly a meeting place for events in the town while today it houses a small museum providing details about the town's history.

The Tudor Moot Hall on Aldeburgh seafront was once situated in the centre of the town.

The name Aldeburgh means 'old fort' although erosion since the sixteenth century has meant that the fort and many of the Tudor buildings and their history have now been lost. Indeed the Moot Hall, once in the centre of the town, now overlooks the shingle beach, underlining how the pattern of the town must have changed. In the sixteenth century shipbuilding was a thriving industry in Aldeburgh, much as it had been along the coast at Dunwich in the thirteenth century. A number of famous ships were built in Aldeburgh including the *Golden Hind* (previously the *Pelican*) and the *Greyhound* which were both captained by Sir Francis Drake. It is also thought the *Sea Venture*, a ship of the Virginia Company, was also built in the town in 1608. Eventually however, with the silting of the river Alde, Aldeburgh's fortunes as a port declined and it relied instead on trade as a fishing port until the nineteenth century.

Today the town's main industry is from tourists and with its decline as a boat building and fishing port it developed as a genteel resort. A large hotel on the front caters for

A fishing boat lies deserted on the beach, a reminder of the fishing industry which played such an important part in Aldeburgh's history.

The Mere at Aldeburgh is a quiet retreat, just a short walk from the sea.

Colourful cottages on the approach to the Town Steps.

The old water pump which once served the residents of Aldeburgh.

visitors today, and although generally peaceful there are clearly parts of the town which come to life in the summer. A short distance away from the Moot Hall along the seafront is the Royal National Lifeboat Institute museum and station, which provides details of the lifeboat and its importance to the town as well as the chance to look at the lifeboat itself on display. There are also daily boat trips from Slaugden Marina with the opportunity to look at the coastline from the sea.

The main street of the town is just a short distance from the seafront and there is a range of shops; the town's fish and chip shop has earned itself an enviable reputation. Approaching it on my visit there is a sizeable queue eager to partake of the delights on offer and I am assured that these are the best fish and chips around. Elsewhere in the town, around each corner or down each passage, there seems to be something of interest and walking back along the main street I come to the Town Steps, a characterful row of houses flanked by the steps themselves. The view of the sea from the top of the steps is quite entrancing and hidden at the side of the steps is a restored water pump dating from 1890, carefully restored in 2007. This was the source of water in town in times past and it

A pretty garden in centre of the town.

The view over Aldeburgh from the town steps.

Seagulls swoop low along the seafront looking for food.

The ceaseless ebb and flow of the sea along the shingle beach.

is hidden details like this which make Aldeburgh such an intriguing place. Today Aldeburgh, although far smaller than in its heyday, still supports a small fishing industry with fresh fish being sold on the seafront .

Benjamin Britten's opera 'Peter Grimes', has the same title as a poem by George Crabbe, who was born in Aldeburgh in 1756, and who clearly provided Britten with his inspiration, as did the sea and the unique character of the town.

The beach is a perfect place for a relaxing and taking peaceful walk with the fresh air and long strand of shingle stretching off into the distance. Occasional fishing boats lie drawn up on the beach typifying the relaxed character of the town. In the distance is the unusual 'House in the Clouds' and its neighbouring windmill at Thorpeness. A short walk along the shore brings us to the intriguing sculpture which is known as 'The Scallop', resembling a large clam shell. The piece was produced as a tribute to Benjamin Britten and provoked controversy when it was unveiled a few years ago, with locals claiming it was ugly or unsuitable, and some called for it to be removed. The Scallop is the work of Maggi Hambling, the Suffolk artist who created this modern structure from stainless steel and today visitors are content to take pictures of what is now an iconic landmark.

Nearby is the North Warren site run by the RSPB with marshland, woodland and other habitats. It is notable for the dragonflies and a wide variety of bird species including hobbies, ducks, swans and geese. In the spring bitterns, marsh harriers, skylarks and nightingales can be seen here.

'The Scallop' on Aldeburgh beach is the work of Suffolk artist, Maggi Hambling.

Boating on the Mere is popular activity during the summer months.

Further along the beach is Thorpeness which, like Aldeburgh, had some industry in the form of fishing in the nineteenth century when it was also just a small settlement. Modern Thorpeness took shape after Glencairn Ogilvie bought the whole area in 1910 and developed it into a holiday village. Ogilvie made his fortune from designing railways around the world but chose to develop Thorpeness as a quiet retreat to which he invited friends. The focal point of the village is the Mere, a large lake, which in summer is busy with children feeding the swans and exploring the water in boats provided for hire. Taking a break by the Mere in the summer sunshine, it is easy to see what attracted Ogilvie to this enchanting place.

Immediately attracting attention is the 'House in the Clouds', a perhaps eccentric landmark but with its own delightful character, something like a house on stilts towering over the trees and heathland. On my trip visitors are clearly enjoying the sight of this unusual landmark. The house itself was formerly a water tower supplying water to the village but was rather different from a bland metal or concrete tower. It was built in 1923 and to make it more attractive it was clad in wood to resemble a very tall house. During the war the capacity of the tower was reduced from 50 000 to 30 000 gallons when it was hit by gunfire and it had to be repaired. By 1972 a mains water supply meant the tower became redundant and today the house atop the tower is rented out to holidaymakers who enjoy spectacular views over the town.

A few feet away and opposite the 'House in the Clouds' is Thorpeness windmill. It is a small attractive post mill and is open throughout the summer, welcoming visitors. Originally it was a windmill used for grinding wheat sited in Aldringham a few miles away and dates from 1803. By the 1890s the Ogilvie family were the millers and in 1922 they decided to move the mill from its former location to Thorpeness.

Amos Clarke of Whitmore's Millwrights from Wickham Market was the millwright in charge of dismantling and moving the structure. The mill was then used as a water pump for the 'House in the Clouds' able to pump up to 8200 litres of water an hour until it was replaced in this role with an petrol engine. The mill then stood dormant and in 1972 the fantail was damaged in a storm, while a fire on the heath surrounding the mill in 1973 caused further damage. Luckily for the mill, in 1975 Suffolk Coastal District Council put forward money for restoration which took place in 1977. Today the mill is in excellent condition and visitors are able to climb inside and explore.

The distinctive 'House in the Clouds' was once a water tower supplying Thorpeness.

Thorpeness windmill originally ground wheat but in the 1890s it was moved and converted into a water pump. It is open to visitors and stands alongside the 'House in the Clouds'.

After looking at these interesting buildings, I am keen to take in some more of the peaceful charms of Thorpeness and walking around the village. Many people are clearly content to enjoy the tranquil setting and the relaxed atmosphere make this the perfect place for those seeking a retreat. There are tennis courts and a golf club for those interested while a pub and tea room provide a break for those seeking refreshments.

THINGS TO DO

- Take a walk through the town, climb up the Town Steps for a view over Aldeburgh

- Visit the Moot Hall and look out for Benjamin Britten's House close by.

- Walk along the beach with fishing boats moored up, visit the lifeboat and take a look at 'The Scallop'.

Chapter 12
LEISTON AND MINSMERE

THE SMALL TOWN of Leiston, today most notable for the ruins of Leiston Abbey, was once a centre for heavy industry in Suffolk. At the end of the eighteenth century Richard Garrett built an ironworks in Leiston and Garrett & Sons quickly became known as a leading manufacturer of agricultural machinery in East Anglia. Initially they were known for producing drills and horseshoes. They later specialised in threshing machines, steam rollers, ploughs and tractors and exported machinery to countries such as Africa and Australia. By the mid nineteenth century the company was employing 500 people and by

The Abbey is now in the care of English Heritage and open to visitors.

*Once an impressive building, the
Abbey was dissolved in 1536.*

the start of the twentieth century this figure had doubled. In 1914 the firm built a railway for the Tsar in Russia and during the First and Second World Wars they produced hand grenades. The factory, however, was never modernised and eventually it closed in 1980, although its significance in the town meant that the decision was taken to restore it as an industrial museum which opened in 1983.

Leiston Abbey is situated a short distance outside the town. The Abbey was originally founded at Minsmere in 1182 by Ranulf de Glanville, Lord Chief Justice to King Henry II and was run by the Augustinian Canons who followed Premonstratensian Rule with duties of preaching and other pastoral work. The site, however, was prone to flooding due to its low lying nature and the Abbey was eventually moved to Leiston in 1363. The Earl of Suffolk, Robert de Ufford devoted the last years of his life to building the impressive Abbey.

After the Dissolution Act of 1536 the Abbey was dissolved and quickly began to deteriorate as Henry VIII carried out his destructive campaign across the country. The Abbey was granted to the Duke of Suffolk, Charles Brandon, Henry's brother-in-law, who used the site as a farm. A farmhouse was even built into the ruins and much later a Georgian frontage was added to the farmhouse. In the 1920s it was extended, giving the Abbey its slightly curious appearance today. Many of the country's abbeys and monasteries are now just a distant memory thanks to Henry's recriminations against the Catholic Church, although the remaining ruins at Leiston provide an indication of how grand the site must once have looked.

In 1928 the Abbey ruins and farmland was bought by Ellen Wrightson who obviously appreciated its significance and use as a religious retreat. When she died in 1946 the buildings and ruins were left to the Diocese of St Edmundsbury and Ipswich. Today the site is managed by English Heritage and is a popular place for visitors to stop off and explore this fascinating piece of Suffolk's past. It is also a venue for weddings and other events which take place throughout the year.

A short distance away is Minsmere, the best known RSPB nature reserve in Suffolk with a large number of wildfowl species taking advantage of the environment on the Suffolk Heritage coast, with Westleton and Dunwich Heath nearby. Avocets, bitterns, marsh harriers, bearded tits and nightingales enjoy residence in the reserve while common terns arrive in mid April with redshanks and ruffs following in June. Nightjars also heard. During the summer there are dragonflies and butterflies and the reserve is known as the best place in the United Kingdom to hear the distinctive and rare booming bitterns. Great spotted woodpeckers can be heard at work and dartford warblers make a home on the heathland with its bracken and heathers, and during the autumn migrating birds and geese pass through.

The reserve was once an area of poor farmland but during World War Two it was flooded as a defence measure and shortly afterwards a pair of avocets were seen nesting on the site, which was the first time they had ben seen in the UK for over a hundred years and it was realised that the site needed to be protected. The RSPB first began leasing and then bought the land and has continued steadily developing and managing the reserve over the passing years. Along with Halvergate Island, a short distance to the south, it is now a very significant area for breeding avocets and many other species. Birdwatchers often come to spend a day in the hides appreciating the wildlife and the simple beauty of the rural Suffolk landscape.

THINGS TO DO

- Explore the ruins of Leiston Abbey

- Visit Minsmere and walk around the site or take a spell at birdwatching in one of the hides.

Chapter 13
DUNWICH

DUNWICH IS A mysterious place. For many, the long beach and peaceful bay make it a tranquil setting in which to spend time, but there is much more to Dunwich. In the summer visitors come to enjoy the pleasant, often almost deserted coastal location. Today it is little more than a small village but its past is full of intrigue and testament to the power of the sea, as well as an illustration of how much the Suffolk landscape has changed over the last thousand years.

Driving up to Dunwich, the surrounding heathland and forest nearby make this a beautiful landscape and the sea of purple heather at Westleton Heath, about three miles away, is a truly beautiful sight at its height in the late summer sun. Also close by is the Minsmere nature reserve run by the RSPB which provides an excellent coastal habitat for sea birds and, for keen bird watchers or those with time to spare, there is ample opportunity to explore further.

Westleton Heath is a colourful sight in late summer.

Arriving in Dunwich, I am first drawn to the beach, the shingle bay stretching off way into to the distance, with Southwold's distinctive lighthouse visible to the north and the distinctive dome at Sizewell faintly visible to the south. With the powerful North Sea waves crashing at the pebbles it is a pleasant place for a walk to take in some bracing sea air. At the edge of the beach there are the remains of a cliff-face but it seems hard to imagine there was ever anything here other than a pretty bay and even harder to visualize that there was once a large and powerful town sited at Dunwich, complete with its network of streets and buildings. Look closer however and signs begin to emerge of traces where the churches and other buildings once stood on the cliff edge, the soft clay soil crumbling easily and steadily falling away with the relentless power of the sea.

Dunwich was a settlement in Roman times, becoming larger with the invasion of Anglo Saxons who sailed across the North Sea from Germany and Scandinavia and settled in East Anglia fifteen-hundred years ago. Unfortunately, the Roman remains no longer exist although its significance and evidence of their settlements and remains which were found is well documented before they were eventually washed away by the sea. At its height in the twelfth century, it is believed to be one of largest towns in England with a population of at least three thousand people and for several centuries it was the most prosperous

The shingle beach at Dunwich.

Miles of shingle beach both north and south of Dunwich provide superb walks.

place in East Anglia and the largest borough in Suffolk. There were even two Members of Parliament at the time of Edward I when East Anglia itself only divided into only two constituencies and at a time when London only had a population of eight thousand; providing some indication of the significance Dunwich once had.

Dunwich's coastal location made it ideal for shipping the transportation of goods and industry. The town was based around the thriving port, transporting wool, corn and other materials to London and farther afield. From Iceland came fish, furs and timber, while the Low Countries exported cloth and France shipped wine. A prosperous boat building yard provided further wealth for the town and ensured merchants and mariners in the town could embark on their dangerous, uncertain, but profitable voyages. At its peak it also had at least eight large churches, a testament to its wealth as well as the whole infrastructure of a bustling medieval town.

The remains of the leper hospital in St James's churchyard.

With this prosperity as a port however, diseases such as leprosy became a problem for Dunwich and the ruined remains of the medieval hospital in the grounds of St James's church on the edge of the village are a reminder of the scourge of this disease. The hospital is approximately 800 years old. In 1175 the church ordered that those with leprosy were not to live in the town but instead in a separate area away from the populace to prevent it spreading. Today these ruins are just a short walk from the beach and are well worth examining further, but remember that in the past they were obviously significantly further inland.

The sea that gave Dunwich its prosperity in time was also to prove its downfall. The harbour was formed behind a long, shingle spit known as Kingshome which faced south and during the thirteenth century it became increasingly vulnerable to storm damage. Records show that in 1286 a severe storm overwhelmed the coastal defences and destroyed two coastal parishes. On 14 January 1328 Dunwich suffered its most serious blow when a powerful storm destroyed and blocked the port, an event which proved fatal

*St James's church which dates from
1830.*

*The salvaged ruins of All Saints
Church. Much of the building fell
into the sea between 1904-19.*

to Dunwich's prospects as it was impossible to reopen the port to ships. The trade went elsewhere and the town's significance as a port quickly declined.

Walberswick a short distance up the coast at the mouth of the River Blyth was quickly able to capitalise and documents show that by the fourteenth century coastal erosion had become an unstoppable problem at Dunwich, rapidly devouring the once great town.

St Michael's and St Bartholomew's churches fell into the sea in the thirteenth century and St Leonard's and St Martin's churches also succumbed to its power in the fourteenth century. All Saints Church was built in the fourteenth century but was closed in 1778 and it too gradually fell into the sea between the years 1904-19. Efforts were made to try and save the church but these proved in vain and all that remains today is a lone column in the corner of the churchyard of St James's Church, salvaged before the rest was lost to the sea. During this time whole rows of streets and the remains of the once bustling town that once stood here were also lost to erosion.

St James's itself is now the only church in Dunwich and dates from 1830, although from its flint construction it appears far older. Close by is Dunwich museum which provides some interesting details and insight into Dunwich's past and is well worth a visit. A few yards up from the museum, the Ship Inn is often busy with tourists and provides refreshments for those in need of a rest after a walk by the sea. For those with an interest in our coastline and the stories and history it has to offer, Dunwich is among the most intriguing of all places to visit.

THINGS TO DO
- Visit St.James's Church with the ruins of the leper hospital and old church and Dunwich museum

- Take a bracing walk by the sea along the long stretches of beach.

Chapter 14
BLYTHBURGH

DRIVING ALONG THE A12 towards Southwold, Blythburgh with its imposing church beside the marshes is an intriguing sight for the passing motorist and with a closer look the village has an fascinating story to tell.

The church of Holy Trinity has for many years been called the Cathedral of the Marshes, and with the tidal lagoon known as Blythburgh Water in the foreground and the River Blyth passing by as it flows out to the sea at Southwold Harbour, it is easy to see why.

The area has long had religious connections and it is thought there has been a church on the site since AD630. Blythburgh Priory was later founded in 1130 by Henry I and the area enjoyed growing prosperity with wool and fish traded on the river bank and with many boats tied up along the quayside. By 1412 Henry IV granted the Priory the right to build the present church. During the fifteenth century several large churches were built in Suffolk as the prosperity of this coastal area grew and Blythburgh was one of a number in the area which included Southwold, Walberswick and Cove Hithe. The fortunes of the region however had already began to decline by the late fifteenth century as medieval shipwrights launched ships too big to navigate their way along the river which had begun to gradually silt up until even the fishermen left. With Blythburgh's demise other parts of the Suffolk coast in turn enjoyed rising importance as trading centres. Over the years the sea walls have been breached by floods, although the area was not reclaimed and instead became a muddy lagoon which today is a haven for wading birds and a variety of other wildlife.

The church was for some time supported by the priory but in 1528 Cardinal Wolsey suppressed the priory and it was then closed in 1538 during the programme of dissolution

The church of Holy Trinity, overlooking the River Blyth.

The River Blyth, once a bustling port but now a tidal lagoon, home to a variety of wildlife.

carried out by Henry VIII. The church consequently suffered financially and quickly began to show signs of neglect.

In 1577 there was a severe storm and lightning struck during a service, toppling the steeple which collapsed into the nave, killing a man of forty and a boy of fifteen instantly. Scorch marks on the church door were believed by villagers to be signs of the devil with evidence of fingerprints in the burns. These marks can still be seen today, adding to the sense of mystery and a darker atmosphere surrounding the church.

It was also to suffer later at the hands of the Cromwell's reformer, the infamous William Dowsing in 1644 who had also inflicted severe damage on the churches in nearby Southwold as well as several others before his campaign of destruction ended shortly afterwards. On 8 April Dowsing and his men arrived on the orders of Parliament to rid the church of all 'superstitious objects'. They tethered their horses in the nave before they went to work and during the destruction they smashed ornaments, windows and statues and even blasted shots at the ornate, carved flying angels which supported the roof beams. Several years later, in 1676 a disasterous fire raged through the village, destroying many of the old buildings and leaving only part of the old Augustinian monastery, the courthouse which had been converted to an inn, as well as the church of Holy Trinity which had a lucky escape.

By the nineteenth century, the church had begun to seriously deteriorate and in 1819 was described as being in 'a very sorry state' with windows patched up with bricks and a shield and angels hanging from the ceiling. Its condition declined still further and in 1847 it was described in a local newspaper as 'mouldering into ruin' and thirty years later the roof was leaking significantly, forcing the congregation to use umbrellas. By the 1880s the Victorian's interest in restoration meant that the church began to receive urgently needed attention and in 1884, after some repair work had been carried out, the church opened again to a congregation. Over the next hundred years the restoration programme continued; new oak pews were made from a beam salvaged from an old Mill at Westleton, windows were unbricked and reglazed and it was gradually given a new lease of life. Inside, the angels on the ceiling still survive and the church has its own unusual feature in the form of the 'Jack of the clock' at the west end of the church which dates from 1682 and signals the start of services. A similar feature survives in the church at Southwold.

In more recent times the church has seen further mysterious events. On 12 August 1944 there was an explosion in the sky above Blythburgh and the remains of a destroyed aircraft fell to ground a short distance from the church. Among the victims of the crash was Joseph Kennedy, the elder brother of John F. Kennedy, who later became President of the United States. The cause of the explosion was never discovered but the church windows damaged by the blast provide an indication of its ferocity.

The church is a local landmark, visible for miles across the marshes and lit with floodlights at night it is particularly impressive to passing traffic and certainly is worth exploring further. With the river running up to Wenhaston and Halesworth the area provides some enjoyable walks.

THINGS TO DO
- Take in the marshy landscape of the River Blyth and visit the church.

Chapter 15
WALBERSWICK

THE VILLAGE OF Walberswick is one of the hidden secrets of the Suffolk coast, a village full of history and picturesque charm and worth exploring. With many visitors heading a short distance further up the coast straight to the well known town of Southwold many bypass this gem.

Looking across the mouth of the River Blyth as it flows into the sea, the harbour is a popular attraction for visitors and a relaxing place for a walk. Colourful boats lie by the riverbank and the distinctive Southwold skyline in the distance seems but a short distance away across the Blyth. A small bridge across the river allows walkers to continue their journey into Southwold with boatyards, fishing boats and other vessels lining the river.

Walberswick harbour grew in the fourteenth century and was a busy port for several centuries.

The picturesque charm of Walberswick has attracted many famous artists including Philip Wilson Steer.

Walberswick has clear Saxon origins and the name 'Walber' is thought most likely to be the Saxon landowner while 'wyc' refers to a shelter or harbour. The village was originally a small settlement but with Dunwich's demise after a severe storm destroyed much of the port there on 14 January 1328, Walberswick grew in significance, quickly becoming a busy and prosperous port. As well as its role as a fishing port with vessels travelling to places as far north as Iceland and the Faroe Islands, there was also trade in other goods such as bacon, corn and timber. Trade continued until the First World War but the port's fortunes had begun to decline and today many of the boats are now used simply for pleasure, moored on wooden jetties along the Blyth.

A short walk away from the harbour is Walberswick beach which is popular with visitors in the summer. With the marram grass and the shingle shoreline stretching off into the distance it is a pleasant place to enjoy the sound of the waves and bracing sea air. The village is also well known for its crabbing and every year the British Open Crabbing Championship takes place with funds raised for charity.

The sea has provided prosperity for Walberswick but over time the village has also been at its mercy, flooding several times during heavy storms. In an efforts to provide some protection grasses were planted and a defensive flood barrier was installed, although part

Walberswick beach proves to be a great attraction during the summer months.

of the village close to the harbour, which serves as a car park, was flooded as recently as November 2007.

The village itself is mostly made up of small brick cottages and a village green close to the river. Along with the floods, fire destroyed much of the village many years ago. A short walk away towards the entrance to the village is the church of St Andrew which dates from the fifteenth century with part of the church now an intriguing ruin. At the time of the Domesday survey 1085 it is known that another, older church existed in the village, situated more towards the marshes and the hamlet of Lampland which once stood nearby. Documents which have survived from the fifteenth century also provide details of its thatched roof, bells and stained-glass windows. With the rising fortunes of the village and the changing taste in architecture the impressive new church of St Andrew was built in 1492 and the bells and windows were transferred. Interestingly the tower is seventy years older and had been built to accompany a chapel of ease which previously stood on the site. The old village church, in contrast, gradually became a ruin by the sixteenth century and two hundred years later the final traces were lost. The parts which had been moved to the church have now unfortunately also gone as Anglicans destroyed imagery in the sixteenth century, the puritan William Dowsing destroying the stained-glass windows in April 1644. The bells were later also sold to fund the upkeep of the church.

The new church endured a difficult time with the rise of the Anglican church and later with a lack of funds during the Puritan period. By the 1690s the parishioners were given permission to demolish the old church and build a smaller one in its place on the condition the grand tower, which served as a landmark for sailors, survived. The collection of ruins at the far end of the churchyard are a stark reminder of the difficult and desperate times many of the churches went through. Its former grandeur was at least comparable to the churches at Blythburgh and Southwold.

Walberswick has long been a popular retreat for artists and with its beauty, history and the surrounding heathland and marshes it is easy to see why. Well known figures such as the actor Geoffrey Palmer, the presenter and writer Paul Heiney and his wife Libby Purves live in the village, as did Sir Clement Freud, grandson of the psychoanalyst Sigmund Freud, until his death in 2009. During the late nineteenth and early twentieth century the village became a mecca for artists and most notable was the acclaimed English painter Philip Wilson Steer. Steer was born in 1860 in Birkenhead, the son of the portrait painter Philip Steer. His father, however, died when he was eleven but his son had inherited his interest in painting and in 1882 he went to Paris to train and look for

The intriguing church of St Andrew. It was built in 1492 but by the 1690s a lack of funds meant the nave was demolished and a smaller church built inside.

inspiration. On his return, he became particularly fond of Walberswick and Southwold and with his distinctive style, he became known as the leader of the English Impressionist movement. Steer visited several times to see friends in the area and painted a number of fine pieces from around 1889 such as 'Girls running on Walberswick Pier' and 'The beach at Walberswick', both on display in the Tate in London and showing some similarity with the much-admired style of Monet. During World War One he was recruited by Lord Beaverbrook, Minister of Information, to paint scenes of the Royal Navy and during the 1920s he increasingly turned to watercolours. In 1931 he was awarded the Order of Merit although by 1935 his sight had begun to fail and he stopped painting in 1940 and died in 1942. A few years after Steer, in 1914, the well-known Scottish architect and artist, Charles Rennie Macintosh, visited Walberswick and enjoyed painting a series of watercolours during an extended trip to the area.

Close to the beach I watch some children crabbing and they enjoy showing me their catches, making the most of their time by the sea.

The surrounding countryside provides habitats for a variety of birds and other wildlife and Westwood marshes are also home to the ruins of an old windpump which once drained the marshes. The windpump is thought to date from 1798 and drained the marshes until 1940 when its working life came to an end. In its heyday the three storey tower mill had a boat-shaped cap, characteristic of many of the mills in Norfolk and had four common sails. Sadly the mill fell into decline, underwent some repairs in 1950 although it was finally reduced to ruins by fire in 1960 and today stands as a reminder of an earlier age. Walberswick has plenty to explore and for many it is one of the highlights of the Suffolk Coast.

THINGS TO DO

- Walk down to the harbour with Southwold in the distance and take in the beach and bracing sea air.

- Take a walk around the village and visit the church of St.Andrew.

Chapter 16
SOUTHWOLD

SOUTHWOLD IS WELL KNOWN as a genteel seaside town with its bright beach huts, pier and picturesque lighthouse in the middle of the town, but with its sense of history and quirky character it feels rather different from any other seaside resort. The lighthouse stands proudly over the town and for many is its most unusual feature. I am eager for a walk along the seafront and the chance to take in the sea air which seems so fresh here. The numerous guest houses cater for the busy throng of visitors during the summer months and it is a popular choice for children keen to enjoy the sights and attractions of the seaside.

Southwold has an interesting history and at the time of the Domesday census of 1086 it was described as a fishing port, with Dunwich, a very much larger and more significant town at the time just a few miles down the coast to the south. Southwold's prospects as a port declined however with the silting of the harbour area and instead it relied on fishing to provide trade and industry. It faced one of its sternest challenges with a ferocious fire in 1659. At the time the town was small and tightly packed together with an abundance of small fishing cottages which consequently allowed the fire to spread quickly. In the blaze virtually the whole town was destroyed apart from a hostelry and a couple of cottages. When the rebuilding began it was decided to give the town several characteristic green open spaces which today provide Southwold with is its relaxed and airy feel. In fact, rather than for aesthetic effect these were used as fire-breaks, spacing out the buildings with the aim of preventing a similar disaster being repeated again.

Southwold faced another rather different threat on 27 May 1672 with the battle of Sole Bay which took place along these waters. Colonial and commercial rivalry between Holland and England, the two greatest maritime powers of the time, led to a number of sea battles

Southwold Lighthouse has guided ships on a safe path since it first became operational in September 1890.

off the East Anglian Coast during this period, including the Battle of Lowestoft in 1665 and Landguard Fort at Felixstowe in 1667 where the Dutch were resisted. Early in the morning the Dutch took the Duke of York by surprise, attacking with a formidable fleet of 138 ships holding a total of 4202 guns on board. However, they were to meet tough resistance from the British which countered with a fleet of 156 ships and 4950 guns and a fierce battle raged all day. It proved to be bloody with many men killed during the fighting and two Dutch ships were sunk, with one captured, and a large number of corpses from both sides were washed up along the shoreline as far away as Harwich, shortly afterwards. Neither side was able to claim a victory and when the Dutch withdrew and did not return to resume fighting the honours were thought to be even.

The line of cannons at Gunfleet overlooking the beach are a reminder of the threats which Southwold has faced by invaders from the sea although they took no part in the Battle of Sole Bay. The cannons were said to have been given to the town by the Duke of Cumberland when he returned from the Battle of Culloden in 1746 and they served primarily to ward off pirates. Later, in 1842, the guns were fired to honour the Prince of Wales, later Edward VIII, on his birthday. Unfortunately during the firing the number one gun exploded, killing the operator, James Martin. The guns were last fired in 1850. During World War One the Germans even considered Southwold a fortified place because of its line of guns and they were buried to discourage attack. Later, at the beginning of World War Two the townspeople were said prevented the guns from being melted down and turned into modern weapons. Clearly the sea is fundamental to the town and its history and character of today.

The lighthouse is the town's most famous landmark and rather unusually is set in the middle of the town, surrounded by houses on all sides, although only a short distance from the cliff top and painted gleaming white. The light stands one hundred feet high and a hundred and twenty feet above sea level and climbing up inside the steep spiral staircase it is possible to appreciate the importance and scale of the lighthouse as well as the opportunity to take in some very interesting views of the town. Owned by Trinity House, it is managed from a control centre in Harwich and, in common with a number of other lighthouses around the country, it welcomes visitors with a guided tour around the building. Fortunately, at the time I visit, it is a beautiful clear day and to the north there are fine views of the beaches and pier, with extent of the scale erosion at Eastern Bavants, a short distance along the beach, clearly apparent. The crumbling of the cliffs into the sea has proved to be a sad tale for those living here, in particular the colourful character of Peter Boggis whose house now sits precariously close to the edge and seemingly destined to be surrendered to the waves in the not too distant future. The whole section of bay, unprotected by any kind of sea wall or defences, has been eaten away significantly in the last hundred years. In the far distance sits the forlorn ruin of Cove Hithe church and the large wind turbine at Lowestoft, about eight miles away, completes the scene. To the south I can see the smaller cottages and buildings of the town and the large dome at Sizewell on the horizon.

The lighthouse took about eighteen months to be built and was begun in 1887 under the direction of Sir James Douglas and, unlike its location today, nestling among rows of houses, it was on the edge of the town at the time and positioned a short distance back from the sea to give it some height and protection from erosion. It was constructed from approximately one and a half million bricks and by 3rd September 1890 it was fully operational, sending out a stream of light to passing ships, and has continued to play a vital role in making the waters safe for sailors ever since. Historically shipwrecks were a frequent problem along the Southwold coast due to the lack of landmarks which proved

An aerial view of Southwold from the lighthouse.

to be a similar problem at Orford a few miles down the coast and during the eighteenth century 283 ships were lost on the waters off Southwold. Sandbanks to the south off Dunwich and Sizewell and to the north off Cove Hithe caused many ships to run into danger and a lighthouse became essential to prevent further tragedy, following the example of Happisburgh Lighthouse in Norfolk which had been built a hundred years earlier. Red stripes either side of the lens served an important role in signalling to ships where the dangerous area of sandbank lies and in navigating a safe course through the channel where only a white light should be visible to the ship's captain.

At first Southwold used a intricate system of an oil lamp which burnt continuously. To produce the flashing light signal necessary for good visibility a shutter system operated the remains of which can still be seen on the climb on the way to the top. A number of round weights were raised up and these then gradually wound down and as they did so shutters over the light would open and shut giving a flashing signal. After a few hours the weights would need to be raised up again and the whole process repeated. These workings, along with the large Fresnel lens were salvaged from Happisburgh's low lighthouse and shipped south shortly before it succumbed to the power of the waves and fell over the crumbling cliffs. In 1938 the lighthouse was electrified and then de-manned. At first, large bowl-shaped light bulbs were used to produce the sufficient light. Every so often these were taken out and rewired and until as recently as 1990 this system was still used. Today three tiny ninety-watt bulbs are all that is required. Combined with the clever design of the lens these are more than enough to provide sufficient light to signal to passing ships up to fifteen miles away.

Another famous landmark in the town, a short distance away is the impressive church of St Edmund's. The original church was built in 1200 by the priory of Thetford but was burned down in a fire in 1430. The present church was then built from 1430-60 using stone from Normandy and Lincolnshire as well as local flint. The large, square tower stands a hundred feet high and combined with the lighthouse is the other dominating presence in the town. Inside, the ornate wooden ceiling gives the church a significant presence, reflecting the former wealth and prosperity of the town, as Daniel Defoe noted from his visit of 1724 which he wrote about in his *Tour Through the Whole Islands of Great Britain*:

> *There is but one church in this town but it is very large and well built, as most of the churches in this county are, and of impenetrable flint... Staying there on the Sabath day I was surprised to see an extraordinary large church capable of receiving five or six thousand people but twenty-seven in it besides the parson and the clerk.*

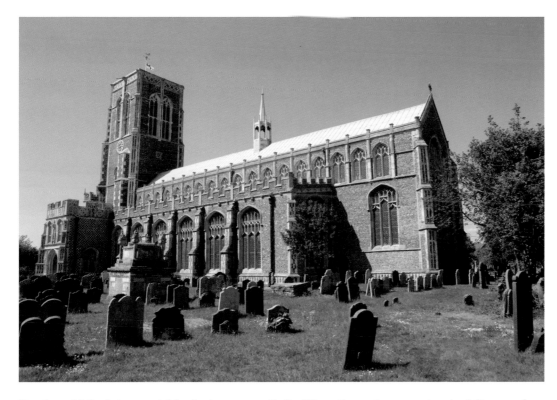

Southwold Jack is a notable feature, a realistic fifteenth century mechanical figure of an armoured foot soldier, made of painted oak and dressed in the period of the Wars of the Roses. Jack even holds a short axe with which was used to strikes a bell before each service or when a bride arrived for her wedding. Unfortunately no ancient stained-glass windows have survived as these were destroyed by the infamous figure of William Dowsing, who came to be known as 'smashing Dowsing'. Dowsing was a puritan soldier from Laxfield, Suffolk and was appointed by the Earl of Manchester in 1643 as the Commissioner for the Destruction of Monuments of Idolatry. His aim was to attack and destroy monuments in the area and during his rampage he visited over two-hundred and fifty churches in Cambridgeshire and Suffolk causing permanent destruction. Dowsing even left a journal noting his exploits and Southwold, like many others, was targeted with no window left untouched. His rampage however, was rather short lived and his commission ended in 1644 when The Earl of Manchester ran into conflict with Oliver Cromwell.

Adnams Brewery stands just a few yards from the church and lighthouse and has been a steady presence in Southwold since the Sole Bay Brewery was purchased by Ernest and George Adnams in 1872. It is thought that brewing first took place on the site in 1396 and by 1890 the business had expanded and Adnams PLC was set up. Adnams has remained independent since then selling beers and ales in pubs around East Anglia and continues to be sucessful with regular trips taking place around the brewery allowing visitors to learn more about the production and types of beers produced.

As I walk round the town its relaxed atmosphere makes this a pleasant place to spend time and explore. The town itself is quite compact and the nearby museum in Victoria Street, which is free to visitors, is busy with those interested in the history of the area. Inside there are details about the local wildlife, lifeboat and coastal erosion which has long played a role in the area. After a look round the museum, the centre of the town with its collection of shops selling mementoes and other items is busy with tourists, and a bustling market is just coming to a close in the main street, much as it has done for many years. A short walk along the high street is the small house where the writer, George Orwell, born Eric Arthur Blair, once lived in the 1930s. Known as Montague House, it was the home of Orwell's parents, Richard and Ida Blair, for several years. Eric Blair was born in Bengal, India in 1903 where his father worked for the Opium Department of the Civil Service. When he was one he was brought back to England by his mothe his father remained in India and did not return to England until 1907. The young Orwell attended a small primary school in Henley on the Thames when he was five. When he was fourteen he won a scholarship to Eton, although he later wrote that he did little work after he arrived but he said his time had been a relatively happy one and while there he made lifetime friendships with a number of British intellectuals. After Eton he began a career with the Indian Imperial Police in Burma but in 1928 resigned and returned to England, having grown to hate what he had seen of imperialism which he wrote about in his first novel, *Burmese Days* (1934).

Why the author chose to use the pseudonym George Orwell in 1933 however was never fully revealed although he returned to Southwold several times in later years to stay with his mother during periods of illness while living in London. It is said he initially wanted to take the nearby River Blyth as his pen name but instead adopted the name of another relatively unknown Suffolk river closer to the middle of the alphabet. As a writer, however, Orwell struggled to make ends meet and lived for several years in poverty and sometimes homeless, working for a time as a school teacher. It was during this period that his health began to suffer and he was forced to give up teaching and worked in a second hand bookshop in Hampstead. In 1936 he married Eileen O' Shaughnessy and during the Spanish Civil War, Orwell volunteered to fight for the Republicans against Franco's nationalist uprising but was shot in the neck on 20 May 1937 and returned home. He then began writing book reviews for the *New English Weekly* until 1940 and during World War Two he joined the Home Guard and in 1941 he started work on the BBC Eastern Service. By 1944 he had completed his well known anti-Stalinist allegory, *Animal Farm* which was published in 1945 to critical acclaim. His wife sadly died that year during an operation. In 1948 he wrote his most famous piece, the novel *1984*, describing the rise of state control and Big Brother. The novel was published in 1949 and shortly afterwards he married Sonia Brownell but Orwell's health had been deteriorating for the last three years and on 21 January 1950 he died of tuberculosis, probably contracted during his homeless days. Sonia continued to looked after Orwell's young son. Today the house is a fairly inconspicuous building with little made of its past other than a small plaque denoting its significance. Southwold continues to be a popular retreat for artists, attracting painters, photographers, actors and writers, and the town is well known for hosting an annual art fair and some of the shops sell a number of interesting books and craft items.

South towards the harbour is the RNLI station and the Alfred Corry Museum which makes a pleasant walk along the beach with the sand dunes and marram grass. The lifeboat station first became active in 1841 when the town raised money from subscribers to buy a boat, the *Solebay* which soon after began service. However, by 1852 this boat was in need of extensive repairs and a new boat, the *Harriet*, was purchased to take over.

The beach at Southwold.

Unfortunately the *Harriet* did not inspire the confidence of the lifeboat men and after struggling with financing the lifeboat for the last fourteen years the society handed over control to Southwold Branch of the RNLI in 1854. A new boat, also called the *Harriet*, began service on 31 December 1855 although while on exercise on 27 February 1858 the boat capsized and the crew, all wearing life-jackets were thrown overboard. Unfortunately the three visitors on board had declined life-jackets and these were drowned in the disaster. Modifications were made to the boat which proved to be successful and the next year Silver Medals were awarded to Coxswain Benjamin Herrington and second Coxswain John Craigie, for their part in saving eleven crew from the *Lucinde*. Craigie was to provide a long and brave service to the lifeboat, retiring after forty-eight years in 1898. The *Harriet* too was to prove a worthy lifeboat and during its thirty-seven years it saved seventy-six lives. The next boat, the *Alfred Corry*, which is on display in the lifeboat museum along with numerous photographs and mementos, took over in 1893. Alfred Corry himself was born in 1858, the son of a copper merchant in Dublin, and eventually the family settled in Wandsworth, London. During his career Alfred became member of the Associate of Civil Engineers but died while only thirty-four in 1892. In thanks for the lifeboat saving his parents at Cork, in his will he left a sum of £2000 to fund a new lifeboat although he gave no directions as to its location and it was decided to use the funds for a new lifeboat at Southwold. The new boat was launched forty-one times in all and saved forty-seven lives, finally ending service in 1918.

Sandunes and beach huts at Southwold.

Eventually in 1979 the boat was bought by Captain John Craigie, grandson of the long serving coxswain of the boat. By 1991 the *Alfred Corry* was in need of repairs and brought back to Southwold where it was restored to its former glory and then put on display. Walking on from the lifeboat museum we come to the mouth of the River Blyth and the harbour with Walberswick on the other side. With the boatyards and colourful vessels moored along the river it is a pleasant place to explore and to glimpse of how the working side of Southwold would have been in years gone by.

As with many seaside towns, Southwold once had a railway which opened in 1879 to carry holidaymakers and some freight (and once even a lion for a circus which was taking place in the town). The railway line connected with the main London to Yarmouth at Halesworth and had an unusual narrow gauge track and it was said to be a rather sedate, if scenic journey. The service continued until 1929. Walking back towards pier the brightly-coloured beach huts and beaches complete the seaside setting and it is easy to see why some like Southwold so much. The sandy beaches however require more attention

Southwold Pier is one of the town's biggest attractions.

than might first appear however, and at least twice during the year large amounts of sand have to be redistributed due to the relentless pull of the waves. The pier itself is not particularly long or old but is considered by many be one of the most attractive piers in East Anglia, and it is easy to see why. It provides an enjoyable place to pause and take in the sea air and the famous outline of the town. The pier was built in 1900 and was originally 810 feet long, designed by W Jeffrey. Steamers frequently called en-route from London to Great Yarmouth but by the 1930s their popularity had declined with the growth of the railway. In 1934 a severe storm seriously damaged the pier and in 1936 a new pavilion was built. During the war, precautions meant the pier was sectioned off to prevent invasion and was even hit by a mine causing further damage.

The pier today, despite its appearance, is rather modern and was given a major refurbishment in 2001, marking over one hundred years since the original pier was built.

Erosion of the cliffs at Eastern Bavants.

*One of the unusal machines
on the pier.*

A new T-section was added to replace that which had been lost in 1934 and it now stands at 623 feet (190 metres) long. Walking along the pier, the eccentric clock with its moving parts and water fountain is a source of constant amusement for the children, and here the shop and restaurant is busy with those pausing to take in the setting.

Walking up the beach the long stretch of deserted sandy beaches makes a relaxing walk and I am keen to have a look at the scale of erosion and the crumbling cliffs at Eastern Bavants and learn more of Peter Boggis. Mr Boggis had lived in the 1930s house over-looking the sea much of his life, with it serving as a holiday home for four generations of his family. In an effort to protect the property in recent years he constructed makeshift sea defences from soil at the bottom of the cliff at considerable cost to himself, attracting much local attention. Unfortunately he carried out the work without planning permission and this in turn sparked a series of fiercely contested court cases between himself and Natural England, a charity, which felt strongly that nature should take its course and with it the cliffs and house close by. During the litigation both sides claimed victory although eventually the ongoing struggle proved too much and the house was demolished in April 2011 for safety reasons as it stood perilously close to the cliff edge, with compensation paid to the family by Waveney District Council as part of its Pathfinder Scheme, put forward by the government to fund demolitions and assisting residents affected by coastal erosion.

THINGS TO DO

- Visit the lighthouse and climb up inside for some aerial views of the town.

- Walk around the town, visit the church of St Mary and Southwold museum and look out for the house where George Orwell once lived.

- Walk along the seafront with the colourful beach huts, to Gunfleet and the Alfred Corry RNLI museum and beyond to Southwold harbour.

- Visit the pier and walk along to Eastern Bavants to witness the erosion taking place.

Chapter 17
COVE HITHE AND KESSINGLAND

COVE HITHE IS WELL KNOWN for the threat it has faced from erosion and the impact the relentless advance of the sea has had on the village, which over the centuries has been washed away, although the intriguing ruin of the church remains makes the village worth exploring.

Cove Hithe is about three miles north of Southwold and arriving down the twisting lane with trees and farmland all around, the church of St Andrew stands proudly overlooking the sea. The mystery and fate of the area seems to be a popular attraction for visitors, keen

The ruins of the once impressive church of St Andrew

The Church of St Andrew.

to take a look at a hidden nook of the Suffolk coast. From the building which remains this was clearly once a very imposing church, much like those at Blythburgh and Southwold in terms of scale and appearance. Today only the tower and shell of the old church survives, with a curious small thatched building inside. As with those other grand churches, this was once a magnificent site, dating from the early fifteenth century. The village, once known as North Hales, was significantly larger and prosperity in the area was reflected in the scale of the church and its grand tower. However, as with many other churches it began to endure leaner times in the sixteenth century under restrictions inflicted by Henry VIII and the church, as with many others in Suffolk was the subject of attack by the Puritan, William Dowsing in April 1644 who smashed stained-glass windows and other objects.

The upkeep of such a large church soon became increasingly difficult for the village people and permission was given by parishioners to dismantle the old church in an effort to save money in a time when the congregation was smaller and worship was a more discreet matter. The roof was removed and a smaller church built inside in 1672. As with Walberswick, which was dismantled a few years later in 1690, the tower was left intact because of its significance as a landmark for mariners with Trinity House keen for its survival along this difficult stretch of coast.

Erosion is the most significant aspect of the story of Cove Hithe and the rate of loss of farmland in recent years, owned by the Benacre Estate, is particularly shocking with photographs taken in the last few years demonstrating the alarming rate at which the sea has eaten away at the soft cliffs. Looking down over the shoreline the view of the sea is a beautiful one although even on a warm summer day the strong winds and crashing waves make it easy to imagine how ferocious the sea can be here. To the right is Southwold, slightly sheltered compared to Cove Hithe, and it is easy to see that with nothing to stop the sea it will continue to eat away at the farmland and, eventually, what remains of the village.

The sea continues to eat away at the vulnerable cliffs.

A short distance along the coast are the small villages of Kessingland and Pakefield. Today the area is a popular holiday resort about three miles south of Lowestoft and during the summer months the caravan parks and chalets are a hive of activity as visitors come to enjoy the charms of the Suffolk/Norfolk border, with Great Yarmouth and the Norfolk Broads nearby. The Africa Alive animal park is a popular choice for the children and the pretty beach provides some pleasant local scenery. Kessingland was once a prosperous port, its name derived from 'Cassing's land', the Scandinavian for 'land of flints' and during the eleventh and twelfth century it was the most significant port between Dunwich and Yarmouth. Today the area continues to be of interest to archaeologists with Palaeolithic and Neolithic tools and objects found along the shoreline.

THINGS TO DO
- Visit the church of St Andrew in Cove Hithe and take a walk to the sea for some superb views and to see the ongoing battle with erosion taking place.

136

Chapter 18
LOWESTOFT

CLOSE TO THE BORDER with Norfolk, Lowestoft is the second biggest town in Suffolk and the most easterly point in the UK. The town, like many others on the coastline grew around the fishing industry, in particular herring, with white fish such as plaice and cod later becoming the main catches.

Lowestoft beach. The town flourished during its Victorian heyday.

At its height in the fourteenth century Lowestoft was a bustling fishing port, the industry playing a major role in the town. After the Napoleonic wars, which ended in 1814, Dutch fishing in the North Sea declined and boats from Lowestoft were able to thrive, the accompanying development of the railway enabling fresh fish such as herring and mackerel to be quickly transported. The number of drifters fishing the waters rose dramatically, from 80 in 1841 to almost 400 by 1900 with an influx of Scottish fishermen and girls helping to unload the cargoes on the quayside.

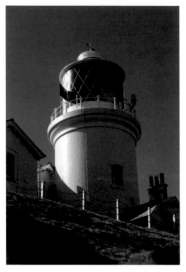

A lighthouse has shone out at Lowestoft since 1670. The present building was completed in 1874.

Fishing methods also changed with trawling becoming more significant. In 1863 there were eight trawlers but by the 1880s there were nearly 300 trawlers fishing the waters. Eventually however, with overfishing, the herring began to disappear, instead more reliance was placed on more on catches of white fish but in recent times fishing, which had provided so much industry in the town, has now severely declined. Today visitors are drawn to the area by the scenery and by the excellent sailing facilities here and on the nearby Norfolk Broads.

Lowestoft has long been a target for invaders and has clear Viking origins, 'Hlovther toft' which the town was originally called, meaning homestead. By the time of the Domesday book in 1068 it had become known as 'Lothu Wistoft' which then eventually became Lowestoft. Its easterly location meant that along with the Vikings, it was a prime target for invasion in World War One, while in World War Two it was a heavily bombed target, the Luftwaffe destroying much of the old town.

The maritime past of Lowestoft is not far from the surface and the unusual lighthouse on the edge of the town is a reminder of the significance and dangers this area of coastline held for sailors. The numerous sandbanks along the coast meant that many ships and cargoes were lost and, as at Orford and Southwold, a lighthouse was essential in ensuring

Ness Point is the most easterly point in the England.

138

safe navigation. Pressure from shipowners and merchants led to the first lighthouses being built at Lowestoft in 1607 by Trinity House. As at Harwich in Essex, there was a low and a high lighthouse and with the two lights in-line ships were led safely through the Stamford Channel, a safe route which now no longer exists due to the shifting sandbanks. By 1706 the low light had ceased operation but after complaints and the danger in steering a clear course, a low lighthouse resumed action in 1730, with a pair operating until the low lighthouse finally became redundant in 1923 with silting of the channel. Changes in technology also meant that the high lighthouse moved from coal fire to a glass lantern system in 1777, this new system visible for up to twenty miles.

Electric light brought huge improvements in lighthouse design and with electrification at Southwold Lighthouse a few miles to the south, it was decided in 1870 to do the same with the high lighthouse in Lowestoft. A new, more substantial building however was necessary for the heavier equipment and the lighthouse we see today was built and completed in 1874. In passing the structure itself looks particularly unusual, hardly any higher than a house and almost like a miniature lighthouse although, viewed from the shoreline, it stands high with its vantage point on the clifftop looking out to sea. By 1974 it was automated and then modernised in 1997 and today it gleams white in the sunshine, offering welcome assistance as it has done for many years.

The large wind turbine, known as 'Gulliver' is an unmissiable presence in the town.

Just along the coast the immense wind-turbine provides another local, yet more modern, landmark which has become affectionately known as 'Gulliver' in reference to its surreal size. It is in fact, the tallest wind turbine in the UK so far and it is only when walking along the Ness Point coastal path, seeing the enormous blades cutting the air, that it is possible to appreciate its gigantic size. Built in January 2005 it stands 80 metres (262ft) high from the base to the turbine hub, and 126 metres (413ft) to the top of the wing tip. With blades 44.8 metres (147 ft) long it is able to generate enough electricity for up to 1500 homes in the local area, harnessing the windy conditions on offer at the most easterly point of the UK. This is Ness Point, marked with a large compass-like design a few yards from the turbine. The wind turbine project, operated by local engineering firm SLP, proved such a local talking point that it was opened to the public on National Wind Day in June 2008 with many visitors keen to learn more, a sign of our changing attitudes to new sources of energy.

As with many other seaside towns along the coastline Lowestoft enjoyed a period of prosperity during the Victorian times, fuelled further with development of the railways. The Claremont Pier, now unfortunately lacking its former splendour, is a reminder of the

The South Pier provides seaside amusements for visitors.

Boats moored in the marina by the South Pier.

Victorian and Edwardian heyday and, as with the piers at Felixstowe and Southwold, the Claremont Pier was built by the Coastal Development Company. Formed in 1898, it ran the Belle steamships, providing pleasure cruises and trips along the coast and up to Great Yarmouth, with stop off points at the other piers along the way such as Southend, Walton and Clacton.

Designed by D Fox and built in 1903 it was originally 600ft long and 36 ft wide and hailed as among the most elegant of all piers. It was then extended with a T-shaped head in 1912 and a pavilion was built bringing the pier to 760 ft in length. The Coastal Development Company however went bankrupt shortly after and the steamer market was an industry in decline, with the last steamers disappearing by 1939. By the time of the Second World War the end of the pier, as with those at Felixstowe and Southend, was sectioned off and the mid part demolished by the army to prevent invasion. Unfortunately with a lack of maintenance the pier had fallen into a declining and derelict state by the end of the war

Oulton Broad is known as the Gateway to the Broads and is popular with tourists and sailors. It is a pleasant place to relax on a sunny afternoon.

years. Fortunately, it was bought by George Studd after the council declined to purchase it and he carried out renovation on the pier, including a new pavilion building in 1950. However, in 1962 the deteriorating T-shaped head at the end of the pier was damaged and washed away in a storm. In more recent years efforts have been made with the landward end of the pier, including a roller-skating rink which has recently opened, providing seaside entertainment for all ages.

There is also another pier near Lowestoft harbour known as the South Pier which from the postcards of the Victorian heyday was obviously rather grand. Originally in 1831 two short piers were built either side of the harbour, known as the Inner North and South Piers, both 500ft long. In 1846 the South Pier was extended to 1320 ft as part of development of the harbour and in later years further developments included a reading room in 1853 and a bandstand in 1884. A new pavilion was also built from 1889-91 to replace the reading room which had been destroyed in a fire, and in 1928 strengthening work was carried out. However the pier suffered in World War Two, just as had the Clairmont, and the pavilion was destroyed. After the war a new pavilion opened in 1956 which was also demolished in 1975. In more recent years it has focused on providing amusements and today it is a more modest, less ornate structure. It also serves as part of the sea wall and defences.

As well as the seaside recreation, nearby Oulton Broad is a popular location. Known as the Gateway to the Broads, it is a picturesque place for visitors, with opportunities to sail and take part in water sports or explore the beauty of the Broads. The Nicholas Everitt park alongside Oulton Broad is a relaxing setting on a sunny afternoon, with boats and swans sailing past and the large converted mill buildings adding a sense of history to the scene.

THINGS TO DO
- Take a walk along the South Pier and seafront.

- Visit the lighthouse, park and museum.

- Explore Oulton Broad and Nicholas Everitt Park.

BIBLIOGRAPHY AND USEFUL LINKS

Books
East Anglia, Peter Sager, Pallas, 2002.
Suffolk, A Potrait in Colour, Mark and Elizabeth Mitchell, 1992, Countryside Books.
The Suffolk Coast, Russell Edwards, Terence Dalton, 1991.
Suffolk, Francis Frith Collection by Clive Tully, 1999.
Suffolk Coast From The Air, Mike Page and Pauline Young, Halsgrove, 2006.
Explore Britain's Coastline, Richard Cavendish, Daily Telegraph Publishing, 1993.
Sutton Hoo, Burial Ground of Kings, Martin Carver, 1998.
East Anglian Landscapes, Ravensdale and Muir, Michael Joseph, 1984.
Suffolk Coast From The Air 2, Mike Page and Pauline Young, Halsgrove, 2009.
The Valley of the Stour, N G Rogers, 1992.
Country Towns and Villages of Britain, 1985, Drive Publications.
Southwold, Portrait of a Seaside Town, Clegg, 2005.
John Constable, Frieda Constable, Dalton 1975
A Possible Roman Tide Mill, Rob Spain, Kent

Booklets, websites etc
Anglian Water, Alton Reservoir Information
www.dedhamparishchurch.org
Dedham/Flatford Tourist Information
www.suffolkchurches.co.uk
Suffolk Archive of Woolverstone and Freston (Ipswich)
East Anglian Daily Times article 1997 (John Blatchley)
Evening Star November 1999
Shotley Parish Council Website www.onesuffolk.co.uk

Harwich Tourist Information
The old lawmower club
www.competitoncommission.gov (Fisons)
Gainsborough House information
www.suffolktouristguide.com
www.visitsuffolkcoast.co.uk
www.visitsuffolk.co.uk
Landguard Fort information
www.heritage.co.uk
www.bawdseymanor.co.uk
www.villagevoices.org.uk
East Anglian Daily Times (5 July 2010).
www.visitwoodbridge.co.uk
Woodbridge Tourist Information
St Mary's Parish Church Guide, Woodbridge
Buttrams Windmill guide, Woodbridge
www.abolition project.co.uk
English Heritage, Orford Castle Guide
St Bartholomews Church Guide, Orford
Sutton Hoo Society

National Trust Information, Sutton Hoo.
RSPB website www.rspb.org.uk
www.snapemaltings.co.uk
Thorpeness, Aldeburgh Tourist iInformation
Dunwich Tourist information and Museum
St Jame's Church information, Dunwich
www.explorewalberswick.co.uk
www.suffolkchurches.co.uk
Trinity House, Southwold.
St Edmunds Church, Museum Information
Southwold Tourist Information
National Piers Society
RNLI information, Southwold.
www.georgeorwell.org
www.holytrinityblythburgh.org.uk
Minsmere, RSPB information
www.historicbritain.com
Lowestoft Lighthouse, Trinity House website
www.nesspointinformation.co.uk
www.heritagetrail.co.uk